Management Skills Series
Successful Business Writing

Successful Business Writing

PATRICIA SERAYDARIAN
AND SHARON PYWELL

Adapted by Dr Pat Haggard

CASSELL

IN ASSOCIATION WITH THE INSTITUTE FOR SUPERVISION AND MANAGEMENT

Cassell
Villiers House
41/47 Strand
London WC2N 5JE

First published as *Writing That Works* and *Writing for Business Results*
by Richard D. Irwin Inc. in 1994

This adaptation first published by Cassell in 1994
© Richard D. Irwin Inc., 1994

British Library Cataloguing-in-Publication Data
A catalogue record for this book is available from the British
Library.

ISBN 0-304-33104-X

Typeset by Litho Link Ltd., Welshpool, Powys, Wales
Printed and bound by Page Bros. Norwich

Contents

Foreword

Many years of experience in the field of management education and training have convinced me that expressing oneself systematically and accurately in writing and coping with the nuances of English grammar are problems shared by a significant number of practitioners from all levels of the managerial spectrum. These particular difficulties manifest themselves most frequently among first-line and junior managers, especially those whose previous training has been essentially of a practical 'hands-on' nature.

Current changes in the organizational structure of many British companies – de-layering and the consequent flatter management structures – have served merely to present these problems in sharper relief. Hardly a week goes by in the life of the contemporary first-line manager in which he is not required to commit his thoughts, ideas or recommendations to paper, often in the awesome knowledge that his literary efforts will, in due course, surface as board meeting papers. Given these trends, it is particularly apposite that the first title in this newly launched series, under the joint imprint of Cassell and The Institute for Supervision and Management, should be devoted to this very important topic.

The authors are to be congratulated upon their achievement in presenting a series of often very complex concepts in such a straightforward everyday fashion, which I find ideal for the busy working manager. On behalf of the Institute for Supervision and Management, I have pleasure in endorsing this book. It should be on every working manager's desk.

G.L.D. Alderson
Director
The Institute for Supervision and Management

Lichfield, March 1994

Preface

Have you ever thought, 'I wish I were a better writer'? Or perhaps, 'I wish I felt more confident that my writing was effective.' Wherever you fall on the scale of writing skills, this book is designed for you.

How can you get the most out of this book? Begin by completing the Self-assessment on page 13. This will help you establish your present position. Then work through each of the 10 chapters. Although the entire book could be completed at one sitting, we recommend that you do one chapter at a time. This will help you focus on a single topic. When you have been through all the chapters, take the test at the end of the book. You will be surprised at how much you have learned.

If you agonize over writing, this book is for you. Do you:

- Take twice as long to write something as you should?
- Know what you want to say but cannot put it down on paper?
- Feel that writing has never been your favourite way to communicate?
- Prefer to pick up the telephone or go to someone's office to communicate information?
- Believe that the documents you write don't get the results you want or expect?

Most people, even professional writers, find writing difficult. No one just *writes*. Writing is not simply getting something down on paper; it is part of a process of working out what you think. You must have a clear, complete grasp of your subject in order to express yourself clearly. Most of us dislike the painful truth revealed by the blank page: some contemplation or research must be done before we can honestly say, *I know just what I think.*

Rest assured, though; your writing skills can be strengthened. Clear, accessible techniques and exercises can improve your writing – this book deals with many of them. This book will give you:

- specific techniques to organize ideas
- guidance to clarify muddled writing
- strategies to get you going again if you lose your train of thought or don't know where to begin

- methods to save time and organize your work habits
- ways to analyse your writing tone and content so that you get the responses you want from your readers

In short, this practical book will give you concrete advice on becoming a better writer.

Self-assessment

How do you feel about your current writing skills? This simple self-assessment exercise will confirm your level of confidence and suggest areas for improvement.

	Almost always	Some-times	Never
1. I can complete a business letter that I am satisfied with in less than 30 minutes.	____	____	____
2. I am confident that my sentences reflect a positive and clear tone.	____	____	____
3. My business memos and letters generate the kinds of responses I seek.	____	____	____
4. I can assess a letter or memo's clarity and organization in one quick overview.	____	____	____
5. I use at least three techniques to write quickly and effectively.	____	____	____
6. My paragraphs are limited to a single topic.	____	____	____
7. I am familiar with several organizing strategies for memos, reports and letters.	____	____	____
8. I set important letters aside for a period of time before my final edit.	____	____	____
9. My readers know what actions, if any, they are expected to take in response to my letters and memos.	____	____	____
10. I know at least two methods of overcoming writer's block.	____	____	____
11. I feel very confident when writing letters and memos.	____	____	____
12. Getting started when writing is easy for me.	____	____	____
13. I feel confident that the format of my letters conforms to standard practices.	____	____	____
14. I always plan before writing.	____	____	____

	Almost always	Some-times	Never
15. I feel sure my opening paragraphs capture the attention of my reader.	___	___	___
16. I gather all my information and check any necessary details before writing.	___	___	___
17. I am careful to state what I want the reader to do.	___	___	___
18. My letters always close effectively.	___	___	___
19. I limit my letters and memos to one page if possible.	___	___	___
20. I limit my paragraphs to single ideas.	___	___	___
21. My electronic messages always get results.	___	___	___
22. The five C's of business writing (conciseness, completeness, courtesy, clarity, correctness) are always identifiable in my writing.	___	___	___
23. I am confident the spelling and grammar in my documents are always correct.	___	___	___
24. I consciously avoid redundant expressions, jargon, clichés and sexism in my writing.	___	___	___
25. I wish I could improve my business writing skills.	___	___	___

CHAPTER 1

The Five C's of Good Writing

> **This chapter will help you to:**
> * understand the application of the five C's of good writing to business writing for success
> * master the application of the five C's

Betty Smith, a medical practice manager, composes many explanatory letters to patients, consultants, and hospital and community care administrators. The nature of her correspondence has taught her to be careful with details. But she still lacks confidence in her overall writing ability. She wonders whether there is a simple set of guidelines that she could use to evaluate her own writing.

Betty would find this chapter very helpful. The five C's are general guidelines to good business writing. If you are careful to observe these in your writing, you will feel your confidence grow as you write better and more successful letters and memos.

DEFINING THE FIVE C'S

What are the five C's that are so important to good writing? As an introduction, they are briefly defined here. The following pages will illustrate their applications to business writing.

Conciseness:	Write the message in as few words as possible.
Completeness:	Ensure that all the information needed by the reader to respond or act is included.
Courtesy:	Show consideration for the reader.
Clarity:	Write clearly.
Correctness:	Check the letter or memo for accuracy of all statements and details.

APPLYING THE FIVE C'S

Conciseness
Write the message in as few words as possible.

Being concise does not always mean being brief. For example, you may write a 20-page report that is concise if it says only what is necessary.

Being concise means avoiding unnecessary explanations. If the added information is not important to the main message, don't include it.

Being concise means avoiding three common writing traps: wordiness, redundancies and long words in place of short ones. Study the examples of each of these below.

Wordiness

First writing: As much as I would like to meet you for lunch on Thursday, I cannot because my seven-year-old granddaughter, Sara, is staying with me until the weekend. I have an 11.00 appointment on Monday, but I think I will be finished in time for lunch. Is your schedule free on that date?

Revision: I am unable to join you for lunch on Thursday. Could we rearrange this meeting for Monday?

Redundancies

First writing: Past experience tells me that our first priority should be consideration of the final outcome.

Revision: Experience suggests that our priority should be the outcome.

Long words

First writing: We need to maximize our profits in the coming quarter.

Revision: We need to add to our profits in the next quarter.

Completeness
Ensure that all the information needed by the reader
to respond or act is included.

Completeness involves presenting all the facts.

- If you ask a person to ring you, include a phone number.
- If you invite someone to a meeting, give the date, the time and the place.

- If you expect the reader to take action, present all the facts that are necessary.
- If you are making a recommendation, provide supporting data.

Study the examples below for a better understanding of completeness.

Missing details

First writing: Please ring me when you reach your decision.

Revision: Please ring me on 0702 225 1990 when you reach your decision.

First writing: Please meet me on Tuesday at 2.00 p.m.

Revision: Please meet me on Tuesday, 15 September, at 2.00 p.m. in the Executive Conference Room at Metro Airport.

Missing facts or data

First writing: My department members simply cannot tolerate the repeated lateness of Janet Adams. My recommendation is immediate dismissal.

Revision: The repeated lateness of Ms Adams (see below) is having an adverse effect on my department members, and I recommend immediate dismissal.

Janet Adams   *Emp. No. 363-89-7878*

Verbal warning:	1.2.1994
Late 5 min.	15.2.1994
Late 7 min.	22.2.1994
Late 15 min.	23.2.1994
First written warning:	28.2.1994
Late 10 min.	2.3.1994
Late 15 min.	5.3.1994

Courtesy
Show consideration for the reader.

Courtesy is self-explanatory. It means using words such as *please* and *thank you* as often as appropriate.

Courtesy also involves keeping the reader's interests and feelings in mind. The courteous letter uses positive words and phrases rather than negative ones.

Even bad news letters can be courteous and warm. When you are faced with a bad news/good news situation, always deliver the bad news first.

Then write the good news, adding emphasis by putting it at the end of the sentence.

Lack of courtesy

First writing: Your response to our letter last week arrived today.

Revision: Thank you for responding so quickly to our letter.

Negative expressions

First writing: You claimed in your complaint letter . . .

Revision: You stated in your letter . . .

Bad news/good news

First writing: I would recommend that you contact Raymond Wright, since I cannot accept your invitation to speak to your group.

Revision: Since I am unable to accept your invitation to speak to your group, may I suggest that you contact Raymond Wright, who is an excellent speaker.

Clarity
Write clearly.

Clarity involves being specific. A clear letter or memo leaves no doubt in the reader's mind.

Promote clarity in your writing by avoiding vague expressions. Say what you mean. Use a specific noun rather than a general noun preceded by one or two modifying adjectives, e.g. 'a trend', not 'a possible development in this direction'.

Resist the temptation to use jargon in your writing. Jargon exists in every business, is understood by insiders, and may be appropriate for in-house communications. However, it is unfamiliar to outsiders and is not appropriate for external correspondence.

You may find that you can improve the clarity of your writing by controlling the length of your sentences. Generally, aim for 10 to 14 words per sentence.

Vague expression

First writing: The change in managers will have a major impact on our sales forecasts. (Will the impact be positive or negative?)

Revision: The change in managers will have a significant negative impact on our sales forecasts.

Vague noun

First writing: The woman bought a new black puppy.

Revision: Susan Marx bought a black spaniel puppy.

Jargon

First writing: We need to interface about the bug in the VDU.

Revision: We need to talk about the problem with your computer.

Long sentence

First writing: Hopefully, I will be able to expedite the dismissal notice to achieve processing no later than the fifteenth of January.

Revision: I hope to complete the dismissal process by 15 January.

Correctness Check the letter or memo for accuracy of all statements and details.

Only you, the writer, can check for accuracy of statements and details. Another person reading your work may be totally uninformed about them.

Be particularly careful to proof-read numbers, such as dates, times, amounts of money and so on.

Make sure the statement says what you intend it to say. Check the usage of similar words, such as *affect/effect* and *less/fewer*. See Chapter 4 for a review of frequently confused words.

Use the spell check feature of your word processor. But remember a spell check does not substitute for a careful reading by the writer.

Inaccuracy of statement

First writing: Everyone at the meeting agreed we must proceed with the project.
(Did *everyone* agree or is a consensus more accurate? Only you know.)

Revision: A consensus of those present suggests we must proceed with the project.

Inaccuracy in details

First writing: We will be closed on Monday 26 December 1995.
(In 1995, 26 December is a Tuesday.)

Revision: We will be closed on Tuesday, 26 December 1995.

Misuse of similar words

First writing: It's only three miles further down the road.

Revision: It's only three miles farther down the road.

Errors overlooked by spell check

First writing: Mary and Peter were to tired to finish there report.

Revision: Mary and Peter were too tired to finish their report.

CHECK YOURSELF

You have just learned five basic principles of business writing. You now have an opportunity to apply this learning by improving the following sentences. Rewrite each sentence on the lines provided.

Conciseness

It has come to my attention that our employees, new and old, have developed a habit of taking extended lunch and tea breaks.

_____

_____

Completeness

Your performance review will be next Tuesday morning.

_____

_____

Courtesy

Your failure to send in your monthly payment upsets me.

_____

_____

Clarity

A comprehensive review of the company policy on smoking will be carried out by the Executive Board.

_____

_____

Correctness

Four months have only 30 days: April, June, September and October.

_____

_____

Sample solutions appear at the end of this chapter.

The following example shows how even a short letter of complaint may fail to apply the five C's of good writing.

---

23 June 1994

Star Engineering
17 Grampian Avenue
Middlesborough TS7 5PQ

Dear Mr Dodds,

It has come to my attention that the copper piping which you have supplied to us recently has not been up to your usual standard. In point of fact, the last three or four shipments have been noticeably inferior.
In my experience of working in this business, this is not only unusual but extremely serious since our clients suffer as a result.
I expect you to take care of this matter immediately.

Yours sincerely,

Fred Newman
Services Manager

This could be rewritten as follows.

---

23 June 1994

Star Engineering
17 Grampian Avenue
Middlesborough TS7 5PQ

Dear Mr Dodds,

You recently supplied us with four deliveries of copper piping which was of variable thickness and strength. I am afraid that this is extremely serious for us, as our clients are liable to suffer as a consequence.
I trust that you will be able to ensure that the quality returns to its usual list standard in the future.

Yours sincerely,

Fred Newman
Services Manager

Chapter 1 *Checklist*

✓ Use as few words as possible.
✓ Include all the information necessary.
✓ Be polite to the reader.
✓ Use clear and simple language.
✓ Check everything carefully for accuracy.
✓ Proofread spelling.
✓ Check again.

CHECK YOURSELF SOLUTION

Page 20

Conciseness

Too many employees are taking extended lunch and tea breaks.

Completeness

Your performance review will be on 9 August at 9:30 A.M. in Room A-25.

Courtesy

When a good customer like you misses a payment, I know something is wrong.

Clarity

The Executive Board will review the company's policy on smoking.

Correctness

Four months have only 30 days: April, June, September and November.

CHAPTER 2

Getting Past the Blank Page

> **This chapter will help you to:**
> - **develop starting-out strategies like:**
>   - **picking the best work times and places**
>   - **visualizing the whole job before you start**
>   - **outlining**
>   - **brainstorming**
>   - **self-interviewing**
>   - **using the filling-in-the-form method**
> - **learn when to use stuck-in-the-middle strategies like**
>   - **walking away from it all**

'Would you write the first draft of a thank-you letter for me?' Jackie Lester's supervisor asked. 'It should take you only 10 minutes or so.'

Jackie knew that this was not exactly true. The last time she was given one of these '10-minute' jobs, it took her much longer. In this case, it took her over an hour to draft the thank-you letter.

Breakdown of task	Time in minutes
Opening a file for the letter	1
Getting the address and greeting set up	3
Proof-reading the address and greeting	2
Proof-reading it again	1
Staring at the blank screen	11
Going to get a cup of coffee	6
Proof-reading the address again	1
Feeling discouraged	9
Making a quick personal telephone call	7
Writing two sentences	10
Deleting one of the two sentences	1

Getting another cup of coffee	4
Writing the rest of the 10-line letter	19
Proof-reading the letter	8
Printing	1

Total time on task: 1 hour, 24 minutes

How could Jackie have avoided wasting all this time? She could have used the starting-out strategies described in the following paragraphs.

STARTING-OUT STRATEGIES

Pick the best work times and places

Certain routines affect your working time. Having a neat desk, your favourite coffee mug or 10 minutes of meditation can determine whether it takes 10 minutes or 10 hours to get something done. Routines that signal concentration can save you a great deal of time if you develop and use them consistently.

Successful people protect and support their work habits. Their work areas fit their personalities and make them feel comfortable.

Very productive people often have an innate sense of timing or have learned when is their most alert time of the day. If they have a slump right after lunch, they don't plan demanding work for the early afternoon. Productive people know what is easy for them and what is difficult, and they schedule their most difficult work for a time when they can give it the most attention.

Not all of us have enough control over our workday to determine when or how we do our tasks. If more control over the work would make you more efficient, it might be time to talk to your supervisor.

Visualize the whole job before you start

Work expands to fill the time available. If you are asked on Monday to write a short and simple report by Friday, you could spend the entire week completing a task which otherwise would have taken you a couple of hours at most.

On Monday morning, Paul Lewis's boss, Richard Lloyd, asks him to write a short article on Jason Boxsworth, a new engineering employee, for the company's internal newsletter. Richard asks Paul to complete the article by Friday.

Paul knows he will have to interview Jason to learn more about his professional background, his personal life and his new role in the company. He will also need a copy of Jason's CV.

In the past, articles like this have run to about 200 words. Interviews have taken about 45 minutes. Paul knows he can get a CV from the personnel department in 5 minutes if Jason does not have it to hand.

Paul knows what writing techniques work for him. He gets his ideas down on lots of Post-it notes and then arranges them on the wall in front of his desk until the article takes shape. Getting his notes organized takes anywhere from 15 minutes to 4 hours, depending on the kind of writing job he is tackling. Writing an article, once he gets going, can take from 15 minutes to 3 days. When a job takes 3 days, typically 70% of this time is spent shuffling notes. The actual writing never takes more than 1 to 3 hours.

Paul looks at his assignment and sees the work breaking down as follows:

Task	Time (in minutes)	Percentage of total assignment
Interviewing	45	25
Getting ideas down on paper	25	14
Ordering ideas	30	17
Writing	60	33
Editing	20	11

Total time for assignment: 3 hours

Seeing the job as a whole and dividing it into its parts helped Paul to keep the time he spent on this assignment under control. As a devoted Post-it note user, Paul put his task schedule on a large note and posted it beside his computer screen. This was a constant reminder to him that the assignment was totally under control.

Outlining

Some people's hearts sink when they hear the word *outline*. They can still smell the dust from the classroom. The idea of squashing their work into neat *A*'s and *1*'s and little *a*'s is entirely unnatural to them.

There are good reasons to begin a writing task with an outline rather than to dive right in. Setting ideas in front of you on paper ensures that important points are not forgotten.

Outlining also gives you a feeling of power that you cannot get when you try to juggle too many ideas in your mind. Some people who stall when faced with a blank page are simply feeling anxious about organizing what they have to say. As soon as words begin to appear on paper in an outline, control begins and anxiety fades.

The following exercise will help you understand the difficulty of juggling several ideas simultaneously if you are relying solely on your memory.

The ABC Exercise

1. Name all the possible arrangements of the letters A, B and C without using a pen and paper.
2. Name all the possible arrangements of the letters A, B, C and D without using a pen and paper.

Time each effort.

Now try both these exercises using pen and paper.

How did you do?

Almost no one can name the 24 combinations of the letters A, B, C and D without notes. With a pen and paper most people can list them easily.

Our brains have limitations: all of us can examine the two combinations of A and B. Only about one in four or five adults can give all six combinations of A, B and C. Practically no one can recite the 24 possible combinations of A, B, C and D.

CHECK YOURSELF

The Private Industry Council (PIC) has approached your company and asked it to offer summer jobs to 50 inner-city FE college students who have never worked in an office setting. Your superior is not sure whether to say 'yes' or 'no'. He has not had much experience with young employees and is nervous about a relationship with an unfamiliar organization. He asks you to write a report that discusses the request and recommends a response to the PIC.

These are the ideas that run through your mind as you consider the assignment:

typist
learning responsibility
time devoted to training summer staff
gaining exposure to professionals and professional job tracks
disciplining/managing young employees
scheduling complications
substituting for employees on holiday
receptionist
public relations
earning money
developing references
mentors
filing clerk
employee response to the hiring – anxiety, resentment of extra
  responsibility?
employee response to the hiring – fresh, interesting challenge?
dress code
service to the community
training and identifying future employees

As you examine this random list, you begin to see that the items fall into categories:

1. How the programme would benefit the company *or* Why we need the programme.
2. How the programme would benefit the students *or* Benefits of the programme to participants.
3. Kinds of work students can do *or* Action plan *or* Departments and divisions most likely to participate.
4. Obstacles, barriers, prejudices – things to overcome *or* Problem statement.

Move the items from your list into the four categories that you have identified as shown opposite.

1. How the programme would benefit the company:

   a. _____

   b. _____

   c. _____

   d. _____

2. How the programme would benefit the students:

   a. _____

   b. _____

   c. _____

   d. _____

   e. _____

3. Kinds of work students can do:

   a. _____

   b. _____

   c. _____

   d. _____

4. Obstacles, barriers, prejudices – things to overcome:

   a. _____

   b. _____

   c. _____

   d. _____

   e. _____

The solutions appear at the end of the chapter.

This exercise illustrates how to begin an outline. Some writers could move directly from a rough outline like this to writing their memo or report. Others would need to embellish the outline. They would proceed to break down their ideas into subcategories and work out all their transition sentences (see page 78), their introduction and their conclusion before writing the memo or report.

Despite the usefulness of outlining, some people cannot manage to write from a formal list. There is no rule that says you must outline or prepare your writing in any particular way.

If you can't work from an outline, you might like to try another method of organization. Here are a few alternatives to the traditional outline method.

Brainstorming

Sit down with a paper and pen (or in front of a computer screen) and record whatever runs through your head. When you feel you have written as much as you can, read what you have written. Cut out anything that is not relevant. Rearrange what is relevant so that related parts are together.

Set your work aside. Come back in half an hour, or half a day if you have more time, and re-examine your writing. Is your main point clearly explained? Have you supported this point with details? Put them in order. Do you have a conclusion? Draft one if you do not. Chop out anything you don't need.

This technique is not useful for all writers and all situations. If you overwrite and don't eliminate superfluous information, this method might not be best for you. As a technique, it reminds you that much writing involves sitting, waiting and churning out words. For some people the only way to get started is to roll along without a critical editorial eye looking over their shoulder.

Self-interviewing

Many of us have trouble starting to write for the simple reason that we are not ready to start. We have not asked ourselves the questions we need to get down to work. Or we have a vague idea of what we want to say, but we have not worked out the details. We cannot record our ideas until we have a clear focus.

If you are in this situation, there are some very standard questions you can ask yourself about almost any kind of writing assignment. If you can answer them, most of your work is done. If you cannot, you will have trouble getting started.

Consider the following questions as you begin writing. If you cannot answer them quickly, you'll need time to give them serious thought.

1. **Why am I writing this?** The answer to this question is the single most important thing to keep in mind as you write and edit. If you can identify your purpose, your hardest work may be done. Whether it is a letter, a memo, a newsletter article, a report, a proposal or a speech, you must have its purpose in mind at all times. Is the document supposed to:

   Explain?
   Persuade?
   Thank?
   Request?
   Analyse?
   Report?

   Remember: if any line in your final document does not further your purpose, cut it out.

2. **What do you want your reader to think that he or she did not think before reading your letter, memo or report**? For example, if you want your boss to allocate departmental funds to buy expensive software, by the time he's finished your memo on the subject you want him to pick up the telephone and order the software because he sees how necessary or valuable it is. Similarly, if you're setting up a meeting, you want the people who read your memo to think the agenda and the people involved are important enough to make attendance a priority. Always keep your end goal in mind as you work.

3. **What do you have to say to your reader to get the desired result?** What was it about that software that made you want it? Line these qualities up and set them down on paper. What could motivate someone to cancel another date to go to your lunch meeting? Whatever the reason, describe it at the beginning of your memo. This question is a good check on your own logic. If you have not done your homework on the software, for example, you will have difficulty describing the features that make it valuable to you. Some people find out at this stage that the software (or supplier, or equipment) that they thought they needed is not really what

they want. Nothing clears the mind so well as having to explain something to another person.

4. **For whom are you writing?** Put yourself in your reader's position. Your boss probably has not been thinking about software for your job. Your colleagues might not be as eager as you are to come to a meeting whose subject is your job's priority, not theirs. Your boss is concerned about your productivity because it reflects on his or her supervisory skills. Therefore, software that increases your productivity is valuable. Your colleagues might not be as concerned about the meeting topic as you are, but if you make it clear that the discussion will shape a policy affecting their work lives too, they will understand the meeting's importance. Knowing your reader also shapes the tone and content of documents. An internal memo to a subordinate will be very different from a letter going out to dozens of people who do not know you.

Filling-in-the-form method

If you have trouble interviewing yourself and are more comfortable with activities like filling in forms, then the filling-in-the-form method might be ideal for you.

This particular method – answering standard questions on a kind of form – works best for long pieces. It might be useful if you have to write an article for a newspaper, a report recommending some action or a report on a project's progress.

To try this method, fill in the following form. It contains a series of statements or points with blank rules after them; it can be used as a standard form to be filled in at the beginning of your work.

The filled-in form represents the beginning of an outline. Now you can proceed to the document itself or you can continue to fill in more details.

Purpose of the document _____

_____

_____

Points that will persuade or inform your reader

Point a _____

_____

_____

Point b _____

_____

_____

Point c _____

_____

_____

Conclusion _____

_____

_____

STUCK-IN-THE-MIDDLE STRATEGIES

Sometimes nothing works. You wade into the middle of a memo and just grind to a halt. You cannot come up with an outline, an idea or answers to standard beginning questions. The simplest memo seems impossible.

For simple memos and letters

Studies tell us that people who do not take regular breaks are less productive than those who do. If you have been frustrated by the same image on your screen for 15 minutes, it is time to change strategies.

Find a way to break out of that helpless feeling. You need to impose change. Here are some ways to do it:

1. Leave your office for a brisk, five-minute walk.
2. Have some toy in your top drawer – juggling balls, a puzzle, worry beads. Take a five-minute break.
3. Close your eyes and visualize a place in which you are perfectly happy. Once you get there, stay put for at least three minutes.

Now come back and face that blank page.

For more complex documents

1. Stand up and walk away from your desk. Glance around. Flip through magazines and stop when some image catches your eye. Look out of the window and over your colleagues' desks. Do this for five minutes.
2. Now pick up a pen and a sheet of paper (sit down beside your desk) and list all the objects that caught your attention – what you saw in the magazine or out of the window or on the desk.
3. Look at your list. Are there any common threads to it? Perhaps you will see a common mood. Or everything you chose might be the same colour or size. In some cases your common threads might reflect back on the document you stepped away from.
4. Go back to your work, bringing your new observations about what was on your mind (or not on your mind) when you got stuck.

Elaine Hoover is a postroom supervisor. She is troubled that her peers in other branches of her company have different standards for acceptable levels of employee error.

She discovered this when an employee from another branch was transferred to her postroom. The employee complained that Elaine's policy of giving someone an unpaid suspension after a third mistake was much too strict.

Elaine told her boss, Mary Lane, that the company should have the same standards at each branch. Mary replied, 'You're right. We should do that. What do you think the standards should be? Write me a memo.'

Elaine asked around and discovered that, indeed, her postroom had the toughest standards in the company. Were they too harsh? What did she think now she knew her standards were different from the rest? She plunged right into the memo, describing her own office's rules, and then found that she was unsure of her thoughts. At first she tried to justify her own standards, then she tried to alter them to match other supervisors' standards. She became confused and stopped writing.

Elaine could not finish the memo. After 15 minutes of frustration, she walked away from her desk. She wandered around, noting the brass number on the building across the street, the list of numbers on a memo on her manager's desk, the logbook for incoming faxes, the graphs in an advertisement in a technical magazine.

Then she sat down and recorded everything that had caught her eye: the street number, the list on the memo, the logbook, the graphs. What did these things have in common? What could they tell her about the way she was approaching this problem?

Numbers. Everywhere she had looked she had been drawn to hard quantifiers. Perhaps this was her strength, her major interest and the key to how she should look at this problem.

Elaine picked up the telephone and started making calls. 'What are your absenteeism rates?' she asked other supervisors in other branches. How many minutes does it take in your branch to get a fax or memo from your office to the recipient? What's your error rate?'

Elaine realized that she was constructing an argument for her personnel policies out of numbers. Not only did her branch have the best-documented client service, but her staff's absentee rates were the lowest. She was not making her employees miserable with her standards; she was making them the best employees in the company. Elaine decided that she could establish a clear link between her standards and her results.

Elaine's earlier doubts about her standards vanished as she found her argument. She reflected: 'At a conscious level I'm not even aware of how many decisions I've made based on number results and how many systems I've set up that are number-driven. But that's my nature. I look at numbers first, always. And for working out whether a system that counts minutes and pieces of post works, there really isn't any substitute for them. I should have trusted my own instincts right from the start, except that I didn't recognize my instincts!'

Custom and habit or a temporary lack of confidence can stop you dead in your tracks as you tackle a new writing assignment. When you shift the spotlight off yourself and the frustration you feel at the moment and onto a random magazine illustration, for example, you may free yourself to continue thinking about the problem in a less conscious – and sometimes more productive – way. Does this method always work? To one degree or another it does. Even if it does not lead you directly to your best argument, it at least offers you an opportunity to interrupt unproductive moods or thought patterns. In ideal circumstances, it can help you jump over what is obstructing you.

Chapter 2 *Checklist*

✓ Personalize your writer's block strategy – not every technique works for everyone. Experiment until you find one that gets you going.
✓ Set up a comfortable and familiar work space.
✓ Find your most productive time of day and do your most concentration-intensive work at that time.
✓ Visualize the whole job before you begin:
    What are its parts?
    How long will it take to complete each part?
    How should I prioritize the component parts?
    Is there any way to avoid duplication of effort?
✓ Find a start-up method and use it consistently.
✓ How you start doesn't matter – it matters *that* you start.

CHECK YOURSELF SOLUTION

Page 27

1. How the programme would benefit the company:
   a. training and identifying future employees
   b. public relations
   c. service to the community
   d. employee response to the hiring – fresh, interesting challenge?

2. How the programme would benefit the students:
   a. learning responsibility
   b. developing references
   c. mentors
   d. earning money
   e. gaining exposure to professionals and professional job tracks

3. Kinds of work students can do:
   a. filing clerk
   b. receptionist
   c. typist
   d. standing in for employees on holiday

4. Obstacles, barriers, prejudices – things to overcome:
   a. dress code
   b. time devoted to training summer staff
   c. timetabling complications
   d. disciplining/managing young employees
   e. employee response to the appointment – anxiety, resentment of extra
      responsibility?

CHAPTER 3

Organizing What You Have to Say

> This chapter will help you to:
> - use mechanical organizing techniques
> - decide how to order your material

Joe McTavish was often asked to draft short reports for his boss. He had no problem getting started. He could sit and write down hundreds of ideas very quickly. Notes and relevant articles would be scattered all over his desk.

Joe's problem was moving beyond the start-up process and *writing* the report. He usually ended up buried in a mass of notes, with a vague idea of what his main point would be but no clear structure with which to organize his notes into a final report. So he gathered more and more information, talked to more and more people and made more and more notes. But he never finished his reports.

ORGANIZING TECHNIQUES

Joe McTavish could have used several techniques to help him move from his pile of notes to actually writing his report. A description of these techniques follows.

Post-it notes

You can put your ideas and points on Post-it notes. Stick them all over your wall and arrange them according to topic and importance. You will quickly see where you need more detail and what you need to put aside.

When you first start putting ideas on the Post-it notes, don't edit yourself. Write down anything that occurs to you. Just getting your ideas flowing is what is critical.

If you are a writer who gets bogged down at this stage of the writing process, decide how many minutes you will allow yourself to 'start up';

when those minutes have elapsed, shift gears and start to edit and analyse what you have written.

Index cards

Index cards can be used in the same way as Post-it notes. Lay out the cards, each containing a point that you need to address in your document, next to one another on a flat surface so you can see them as a coherent group of related ideas. Then prioritize and group the cards.

Headlines

If you have trouble shaping a memo or report, try using bold headlines. Headlines act as abbreviated topic sentences, giving the reader a quick overview of the contents of your report or memo.

Headlines are tailored to fit individual documents, so there are no standard ones for all situations. Think of headlines as a listing of the ideas your reader must know or consider.

Be willing to tailor the headlines of a report or memo to the situation. A progress report for a job that is going smoothly, for example, will have different headlines from a report for a job that is not going well. Despite individual differences, however, some patterns do exist. Here are some common subject areas for headlines.

Kind of document	Subject areas that get headlined
Progress report	Background information
	Problem statement
	Achievements to date
	a. in chronological order
	b. in order of importance
	c. in order of responsible division/people
	Remaining tasks
	Budget information, if relevant
	Recommendations for action/changes
	Summary
Procedure change report	Background information
	Rationale for making changes
	Recommended change
	Repercussions of change

	Implementation issues
	Summary
Work order	Work description
	Rationale
	Responsible division (or, if an outside supplier is needed, necessary qualities of supplier)
	Time-scale
	Budget
Recommendation report	Problem description
	Recommended solution(s)
	Rationale
	Action plan
	Predicted challenges
	Summary
Meeting announcement	Time and place
	Personnel involved
	Purpose of meeting
	Preparation (if any) for meeting
	Follow-up actions requested (if any)

These headlines can act as starting-points for your outline, and remain in the final report as organizing signposts. Put them in boldface or a larger type size or a different colour. Then fill in the blanks beneath them, returning later to polish and edit a final version.

ORDERING THE PARTS

Order by importance

Ordering according to importance is probably the most common way to organize business documents. The reason is very simple – the writer wants to begin with his or her central idea. This ensures that:

- The reader will not be misled or confused about the document's purpose.

- The busy reader will get the most important information, even if he or she cannot read every word.
- The busy reader will know immediately whether this document must be read.

In a memo recommending that a company participates in the Private Industry Council's (PIC) summer employment programme (from Chapter 2), the writer would order what he or she has to say as follows:

1. Initial paragraph recommending company participation.
2. Strongest defence of the opinion, describing benefits to the company if it participates.
3. Second strongest defence, describing benefits to the students employed.
4. Description of where the students would fit in the company and what kinds of jobs they could do.
5. Paragraph positioned at the end to address problems that could arise as recruitment for the programme begins.
6. Concluding paragraph, restating the position.

The order of this memo displays the information the reader wants right up front – the answer to the question, what should we do? It then defends the recommendation with a 'why' statement. Just as important, it anticipates questions and resistance by acknowledging them and treating them as manageable situations.

Order by chronology

Work plans, explanations of complex series of incidents, instructions on how to do a task or follow a procedure – these are examples of writing tasks that are best ordered chronologically.

This technique can be used in many situations. Here is how it might look when applied to our PIC programme:

Date	Action
June 1993	Interview potential student employees.
	Arrange meeting with participating department heads to explain the programme.
	Run small group sessions with employees to help them understand the programme's goals and to air concerns.
	Select and match mentors.

	Hold press conference to announce the programme publicly and explain our involvement.
July 1993	Place new employees in the postroom, the copy centre, or word processing.
	Mentors meet their students weekly.
August 1993	Evaluate student performance.
September 1993	Meet PIC staff to evaluate programme and modify as needed.
	Issue press releases on programme's success.
	Make job offers, if appropriate, to successful students who participated in the summer programme.

Order by sequence

Ordering by sequence is a particularly good method for instructions, work plans, and other communications that demand step-by-step explanation. A sequentially organized report related to the PIC programme might look something like this:

Instructions to mentors working with PIC placements

1. Attend training sessions for mentors to get a better idea of what to expect and what duties are involved.
2. Hold an initial meeting with your student during the second week of July and each week thereafter for the rest of his or her employment here.
3. Advise students on work issues, help them understand company procedures and, if necessary, act as their intermediaries and advocates with their supervisors.
4. Work with students' immediate supervisors to draft evaluation of their work.
5. Complete final programme report and submit to Personnel.

Order by comparison

Comparing different positions is yet another way to organize material. Suppose that you are comparing A and B. You can organize a report or memo by alternating paragraphs on A with paragraphs on B. Categories of comparison might be distinguished by bold headlines. If A were *we should hire PIC students* and B were *we should not hire PIC students,* your memo might look like this:

First paragraph: How the company could benefit from hiring PIC students

Second paragraph: Possible opposition to this plan

Third paragraph: Solutions to the opposition

Fourth paragraph: How students and employees would benefit from the programme

Concluding paragraph: We should take part in the programme.

Order by spatial organization

In some situations, the most effective way to organize material is spatially. For example, if you are describing a complex tool, you can describe its parts based on how they are actually attached to each other, starting from the left and working to the right. You would show the parts as they exist spatially, one after the other.

CHECK YOURSELF

Helen Spencer works for a company that provides copy services to businesses. Helen's company actually sets up a copy centre in its clients' offices, brings in the equipment and staff and runs the centre.

Helen runs a copy centre in an insurance company, and she is in trouble. Francis Jessup, the insurance company's administrator, has told her that he is extremely unhappy because Helen's company promised him that there would be five people covering the copy machines. The last two times Francis entered the copy centre only three people were visible. Helen knows that one of the missing employees was sick and the other was delivering emergency jobs to people who had brought them in at the last minute.

Helen also knows that she has never missed a deadline and that she maintains very good quality control over her centre's work. She is adequately staffed, but she has to prove this to the client.

'Your contract ends in two months, and I'm offering this job for other suppliers to bid on. You'd better get together a proposal for me, because I'm not so sure that you're the best company to run our copy centre,' Francis tells her.

Helen must sit down with her supervisor and write a proposal to the insurance company now, to convince the unhappy administrator that she and her staff do offer the best service at the most economical cost.

A draft of the proposal's layout is shown below in random order. Refer to the pages by the letters that appear in the upper right-hand corner of each page. How should Helen order the pages for her final memo? Fill in the page letters next to the numbers that appear opposite.

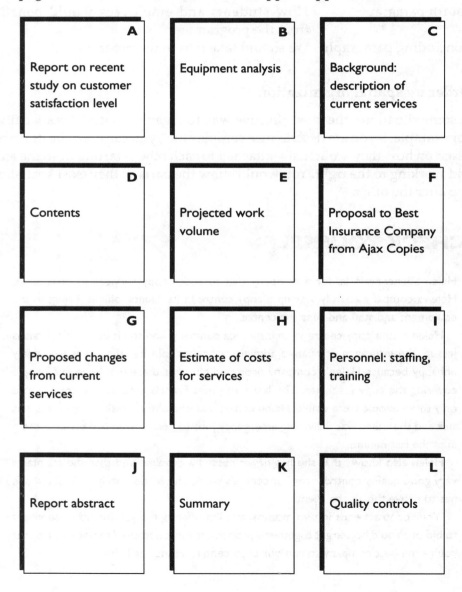

A	B	C
Report on recent study on customer satisfaction level	Equipment analysis	Background: description of current services

D	E	F
Contents	Projected work volume	Proposal to Best Insurance Company from Ajax Copies

G	H	I
Proposed changes from current services	Estimate of costs for services	Personnel: staffing, training

J	K	L
Report abstract	Summary	Quality controls

1. _____   7. _____

2. _____   8. _____

3. _____   9. _____

4. _____   10. _____

5. _____   11. _____

6. _____   12. _____

The solution appears at the end of the chapter.

Chapter 3 *Checklist*

✓ Organizational skills are learned through practice.
✓ Try different ways to get organized:
    Post-it notes
    index cards
    headlines
    traditional outlines
✓ Base your organization on proven methods:
    by importance
    by chronological order
    by sequential order
    by comparison
    by spatial organization
✓ Find an image that gives shape to your thought and use it to organize your ideas.

CHECK YOURSELF SOLUTION

Page 43

This exercise has several acceptable solutions. Sections such as 'Report on recent study on customer satisfaction level' could appear at the beginning, middle or end of the proposal – but in this case Helen knows that she has never missed a deadline and that customer satisfaction is high. She needs this fact to be right up front since her contact person is implying that her staffing levels are affecting the quality of service her company offers.

Francis has specifically questioned the number of people Helen has on the premises, so a section titled 'Personnel: Staffing, Training' was included and placed before the discussion of equipment needs. If the client had been concerned about adequacy of equipment, this order would have been reversed. Helen also knows her quality control systems are particularly good, so she invents and includes the section, 'Quality Controls'.

A section on 'Background' is typically the first in a proposal, but Helen and her boss feel that it is important, given their vulnerable position, to establish the strength of their services before they review the extent of their services. The client already knows what they do – he is questioning how well they do it.

Here is one possible solution.

1. D	**7.** C
2. J	**8.** G
3. F	**9.** E
4. A	**10.** B
5. I	**11.** H
6. L	**12.** K

CHAPTER 4

Using the Right Word

This chapter will help you to:
- feel confident that every word is spelled correctly
- recognize the most frequently misspelled words in business writing
- use correct grammar, recognizing the four areas where errors are most likely to occur:
    change in tense and person
    agreement of subject and verb
    agreement of pronoun and antecedent
    possessives

FREQUENTLY MISSPELLED WORDS

Did you know that many of the spelling errors that appear in business writing occur within the same few words?

Knowing these words and their trouble spots can help you eliminate potential spelling errors from your writing. Listed here are 25 of the most frequently misspelled words. Do you recognize any that cause you problems? Circle those words.

accommodate	achievement	acknowledgement
analysis	benefited	calendar
commitment	convenient	criticism
description	develop	embarrass
extension	judgement	loose
occurrence	possession	precede
privilege	proceed	recommend
separate	similar	supersede
surprise		

You can spell!

The key to improving your own spelling is to know what words you tend to misspell. When you identify the word, isolate the trouble spot.

The spelling problems in these words tend to be the same for most people. Look at the list below. The trouble spot in each word is underlined. Note especially the trouble spot in the words that you circled.

accommodate	achievement	acknowledgement
analysis	benefited	calendar
commitment	convenient	criticism
description	develop	embarrass
extension	judgement	loose
occurrence	possession	precede
privilege	proceed	recommend
separate	similar	supersede
surprise		

FREQUENTLY CONFUSED WORDS

Many similar words in our language cause even the most careful writer to pause. For example, when do you use *accept* or *except*, or *to, too* or *two*? Being able to distinguish between these similar words ensures the accuracy of your writing.

Since the spell checker on your word processor will not highlight these words, it is very important for you to know how each one is used.

Look at the following list of frequently confused words. Review the word, its definition and its use in a sentence.

accept, except:
Accept means to receive something; except means to exclude.
> I cannot <u>accept</u> your explanation.
> Everyone <u>except</u> the patient was pleased.

affect, effect:
Affect means to influence; effect (as a noun) means a result; effect (as a verb) means to bring about.
> Will the change <u>affect</u> your plans?
> The <u>effects</u> were immediately noticeable.
> How can we <u>effect</u> this change in policy?

all ready, already:

All ready means completely prepared; already means previously.

> Are you <u>all ready</u> for your presentation?

> It's <u>already</u> been done.

all right, alright:

All right means satisfactory; alright is non-standard English and should be avoided.

> The schedule is <u>all right</u> with me.

beside, besides:

Beside means next to; besides means in addition to.

> The printer is <u>beside</u> the desk.

> <u>Besides</u> Mr Klein, who is not coming?

ensure, insure:

Ensure means to make certain; insure means to protect against loss.

> The added step will <u>ensure</u> success.

> Is your car adequately <u>insured?</u>

farther, further:

Farther refers to physical distance; further means additional. (In informal usage, these are often used interchangeably.)

> Devon is <u>farther</u> west than Dorset.

> Do you need <u>further</u> information?

few, less:

Fewer refers to number; less refers to degree.

> <u>Fewer</u> than ten responded.

> It occurred <u>less</u> than six months ago.

practice, practise:

Practice is the noun; practise is the verb.

> It is time to put this idea into <u>practice.</u>

> <u>Practise</u> what you preach.

principal, principle:

Principal means main or first in importance or the head of a college; principle means rule.

> The <u>principal</u> cause was unemployment.

> It's a matter of <u>principle.</u>

> The <u>principal</u> welcomed the new students.

some time, sometime, sometimes:
Some time means a period of time; sometime means at a vague, unspecified time; sometimes means occasionally.

I will need <u>some time</u> to do my work.

I plan to revisit Russia <u>sometime.</u>

<u>Sometimes</u> I wish I were young again.

than, then:
Than means compared to; then means at that time.

Let's meet today rather <u>than</u> next week.

I plan to visit the project <u>then.</u>

CHECK YOURSELF

Practise using some of these frequently confused words by completing the following sentences.

principal/principle   Marianne was recently promoted to _____ of the college.

some time/sometime/   _____ we forget that it requires
sometimes

    _____ to learn to use new software.

fewer/less   Would we have _____ problems if we

    had_____employees?

affect(s)/effect(s)   The _____ of the devastating hurricane

    will _____ hundreds of residents for many years.

ensure/insure   Our goal is to _____ the success of the project.

than/then   If you had been given a choice _____, would

    you have chosen to move rather _____ to stay?

accept/except   I simply cannot _____ the job offer at that salary.

all ready/already   We are _____ past our deadline.

                          Are you _____ to defend our position?

Solutions are at the end of the chapter.

USING CORRECT GRAMMAR

Like common spelling errors, grammatical errors in business writing often occur in one of four categories:

1. Change in tense and person
2. Agreement of subject and verb
3. Agreement of pronouns and their antecedents
4. Possessives

Understanding each of these and watching out for them in your own writing will go a long way towards establishing your reputation as a careful writer.

Change in tense and person

Even the mention of *tense* strikes fear in many writers, perhaps including yourself. You may recall a former English teacher speaking a language you never understood: past, present and future tenses; past and present participles; and even perfect and pluperfect tenses.

    This discussion will eliminate the jargon of tense usage and help you spot the most obvious misuse of tense in your own writing. Let's look at some examples.

Shift in verb tense

First writing: We were balancing our books. Suddenly the lights go out.

Revision: We were balancing our books. Suddenly the lights went out.

The verbs in the first writing shift from the past to the present. Both verbs in the revised sentence are in the past.

Shift in person

First writing:	You need to be aware of potential errors that keep our work from being acceptable.
Revision:	You need to be aware of potential errors that keep your work from being acceptable.
	We need to be aware of potential errors that keep our work from being acceptable.

In the first writing, the voice shifts from the second person (you) to the first person plural (our). Two revisions are shown; the one that conveys the intended meaning will be preferable.

Agreement of subject and verb

You must remember one simple guideline:

> ### The subject and verb must agree in number.
> If you use a singular subject, use a singular verb. If you use a plural subject, use a plural verb.

Lack of agreement

First writing:	Each one are eligible for the award.
Revision:	Each one is eligible for the award.

Your errors in agreement are not likely to be that obvious. The following pointers will help you refine your skill in agreement.

- When intervening words appear between the subject and the verb, identify the simple subject.

  Each one of the employees is eligible for the award.

  One is the simple, singular subject; therefore, the correct verb is the singular *is*.

- *There* or *here* is never the subject of the sentence. Find the simple subject elsewhere in the sentence and select the verb that agrees with it.

  There were 70 pensioners at the annual luncheon.

  The simple, plural subject is **pensioners**, the plural **were** agrees with it.

- *Each, every, many a* and the indefinite pronouns take singular verbs.

  Many a young man wishes he had studied harder.

  Everybody thrives on compliments.

  The singular verbs **wishes** and **thrives** agree with the singular subjects.

- When subjects are joined by *either/or* or *neither/nor*, the verb agrees with the subject closer to it.

  Neither the president nor his assistants agree with the new policy.

  Assistants is nearer the plural verb *agree*.

Agreement of pronouns and their antecedents

You also must remember one rule about the agreement of pronouns and antecedents:

Pronouns must agree with their antecedents.
The antecedent is simply the word for which the pronoun stands.

The technician forgot one of his important tools.

His is the pronoun; *technician* is the antecedent.

Agreement of pronouns and antecedents must occur in two contexts:
- Agreement in number. Choose a singular pronoun for a singular antecedent; choose a plural pronoun for a plural antecedent.
- Agreement in gender. When the antecedent is specifically male or female, make sure the pronoun agrees with it. It is often the case that the antecedent could refer to either or both sexes. Sexist references are unacceptable in today's business environment. The examples below will help you avoid this.

Lack of agreement in number

First writing:	Every one of the young women forgot their sales manuals.
Revision:	Every one of the young women forgot her sales manuals.
First writing:	Neither Christopher nor Steven wishes to give up their personal secretary.
Revision:	Neither Christopher nor Steven wishes to give up his personal secretary.

Lack of agreement in gender

First writing:	Each instructor will write his own evaluation.
Revision:	Each instructor will write his/her own evaluation.
Preferred revision:	All instructors will write their own evaluation.

Rewriting the sentence is often the best way to eliminate sexism.

Possessives

An easy-to-remember rule will help you to form possessives correctly:

The apostrophe

If the word does not end in *s*, add *'s*. If the word already
ends in *s*, add the apostrophe only.

Words not ending in s

Base word	Possessive form
employer	employer's
assistant	assistant's
director	director's
women	women's
day	day's

Words ending in s

Base word	Possessive form
typists	typists'
ladies	ladies'
managers	managers'
girls	girls'
weeks	weeks'

Also consider the following when forming possessives.

- When the base word ends in *s*, add *'s* when you pronounce the additional syllable. Add only the apostrophe if you do not pronounce the added syllable.

the actress's costume	Boots' warehouse
Thomas's new house	Mr James' assistants

- Some terms are plural descriptive terms rather than possessives. Do not add an apostrophe to these.

  the Fire Brigades Union
  The Publishers Association

- An apostrophe is also used when forming contractions such as *isn't*, *can't*, *won't*. Remember that *it's* is the contraction of *it is* and that the possessive *its* does not *ever* need an apostrophe!

- Avoid the redundant 'greengrocer's possessive' in plurals – apple's, pear's and banana's.

CHECK YOURSELF

You have completed a quick review of four grammatical points that need to be considered by the business writer. You can now apply what you have learned to the following sentences. Read each sentence and correct it as appropriate, either by changing a word or phrase or by rewriting the sentence.

Change in tense

The staff meeting began promptly at 9 A.M.; at 9:45 A.M. Constance strolls in.

_____

Agreement of subject and verb

Neither the controller nor the analyst want to change the current system.

_____

Agreement of pronoun and antecedent

The surgeon must be dedicated to his task.

_____

Possessives

When will your boss' monthly sales report be ready?

_____

Sample solutions are at the end of the chapter.

Read the following letter. The contents are basically good. However, the letter's effectiveness is lost through little errors. Correct them, referring to the preceding pages as necessary. A sample solution is at the end of the chapter.

---

17 August 1994

Marty Monk
Managing Director
Showtime Theatricals
9 Sion Place
London W14 2SJ

Dear Marty,

Thanks for confirming our commitment to participate in the December pantomime. Each of our principle performers are already to studying their roles. Your enthusiasm has captured us, to!

Its such an exciting time here. We are one of the sponsors of the Physically Disabled Children's Day events in Hyde Park on 15 September. I recall that you have had a keen interest in this in the passed. Julie was speaking at our planning session last Thursday when the lights go out. Never a dull moment – or a blank space in the diary!

Everyone sends his regards. I'll be in touch very soon.

Yours sincerely,

Esther Roland
Scheduling Director

jek

Chapter 4 *Checklist*

✓ Recognize misspelling.
✓ Watch out for:
    change in tense and person
    disagreement of subject and verb
✓ Use the apostrophe correctly.

CHECK YOURSELF SOLUTIONS

Page 50

Marianne was recently promoted to **principal** of the college.

Sometimes we forget that it requires **some time** to learn to use new software.

Would we have **fewer** problems if we had **fewer** employees?

The **effect** of the devastating hurricane will **affect** hundreds of residents for many years.

Our goal is to **ensure** the success of the project.

If you had been given a choice **then**, would you have chosen to move rather **than** to stay?

I simply cannot **accept** the job offer at that salary.

We are **already** past our deadline. Are you **all ready** to defend our position?

Page 55

Change in tense
The staff meeting began promptly at 9 A.M.; at 9:45 A.M. Constance strolled in.

Agreement of subject and verb
Neither the controller nor the analyst wants to change the current system.

Agreement of pronoun and antecedent
Surgeons must be dedicated to their task.

Possessives
When will your boss's monthly sales report be ready?

Page 56

17 August 1994

Marty Monk
Managing Director
Showtime Theatricals
9 Sion Place
London W14 2SJ

Dear Marty,

Thanks for confirming our commitment to participate in the December pantomime. All our principal performers are already studying their roles. Your enthusiasm has captured us, too!

It's such an exciting time here. We are one of the sponsors of the Physically Disabled Children's Day events in Hyde Park on 15 September. I recall that you have had a keen interest in this in the past. Julie was speaking at our planning session last Thursday when the lights went out. Never a dull moment – or a blank space in the diary!

Everyone sends regards. I'll be in touch very soon.

Yours sincerely,

Esther Roland
Scheduling Director

jek

CHAPTER 5

Defining Good Business Writing

This chapter will help you to:
- **keep your sentences brief and simple**
- **use a short word or phrase rather than a long one**
- **choose active verbs instead of passive ones**
- **assume a tone that conveys confidence in yourself and respect for your reader**
- **feel confident about what you are saying by knowing your facts well**

The difference between successful and unsuccessful writing lies almost entirely in how clearly your ideas are presented. Clarity is actually the end product of several writing skills – good grammar, directness, brevity, specificity and a confident tone.

If your sentences require two or three readings to be understood, your reader will be frustrated. All the persuasive data or language in the world will not convince your reader if he or she has decided that you cannot think.

Effective writing skills will help you accomplish your goals and build strong working relationships. They are one of business's most powerful tools.

Many people believe that conversational English and written English should be dramatically different. This belief is not necessarily well founded with respect to business English. A writing style that resembles a lecturing professor or an expert who uses five-syllable words will not make the writer seem more intelligent – it will frustrate readers and put a barrier between them and the writer. Good business writing does just the opposite. It makes readers feel confident that they understand and can respond and it contributes to smooth working relationships.

As you edit your sentences, imagine yourself speaking them out loud.

Write as though you were talking directly to a person sitting across a table from you.

WHERE DO WE GO WRONG?

Why do intelligent, experienced people use unclear language? Some common reasons include:

1. **Being honestly misguided.** Most of us remember a teacher who refused to allow any sentence to end with a preposition, even if that meant writing, 'That is the kind of language up with which I shall not put'. Some teachers sincerely believe that a heavy, academic style is desirable. But as they say in the song, 'It ain't necessarily so'.
2. **Not giving the work enough time or attention**. Finding the shortest, simplest way to say something is actually more difficult than just rambling. Some writers need to set a complex letter or memo aside for hours or a day in order to edit it objectively a final time. Outlining, reading material aloud and reworking – all are necessary components of fine writing that demand time and concentration, particularly if we do not write on a regular basis.
3. **Concealing weak material.** If people are unsure of themselves, they sometimes believe that drawing attention to the language instead of the ideas may hide badly thought-out ideas. This approach never works.
4. **Trying to avoid responsibility.** Some people use the passive voice to sidestep facts. When an administrator writes, 'The invoices appear to have missed their filing date', she or he is using the passive voice to avoid naming the person who made the error and describing how the error was made.

What price do we pay for ignorance, inattention, anxiety and evasion?

Inattention and ignorance. The writer who uses muddy or inaccessible language also appears muddy and inaccessible. In many work situations what we write makes the most lasting impression on our colleagues and they will judge us accordingly.

Anxiety. Some readers will quickly see that anxious writers do not understand their subject and other readers will simply be put off by the writing's complexity.

Evasion. The department or organization that cannot honestly address its errors will never be able to correct them.

KEEP SENTENCES BRIEF AND SIMPLE

Keep your sentences brief and simple, even if you must chop a long sentence into two or more shorter ones. As a rule of thumb, *put one idea in one sentence*. Like most good rules, this is not hard and fast. Sentences should vary in length and vary in rhythm. Your goal is not to turn out quick-fire, homogeneous little sentences, but to stick to what you need to say and go no further.

Here is an example of a sentence that lost its way when it tried to move in two directions at once:

> With regard to all the aforementioned problems about getting to work stations long after the standard time, the supervisors recommend staggering shifts and they do not want to use formal reprimands as part of the solution process right now.

The writer here discusses two subjects, lateness and disciplinary action, in one sentence. The end result is to reduce each point's impact.

A more effective version of this sentence might read:

> The supervisors recommend staggering shifts to reduce late arrivals at work stations. They feel that formal reprimands are not the best immediate solution to the problem.

CHECK YOURSELF

Rewrite the following sentences, restructuring them for clarity.

1. David wants to cut down on time spent managing telemarketers and thinks that they aren't evaluated often enough.

_____

_____

2. I do not believe that the equipment was shipped on time and the invoicing was not even co-ordinated with the ordering process.

_____

_____

Sample solutions appear at the end of the chapter.

USE A SHORT WORD OR PHRASE RATHER THAN A LONG ONE

Most of us have at some time received a memo containing a sentence like this one:

> In the spirit of collegiality with commitment towards maximizing involvement in the exploration and resolution of issues and needs confronting this Division in response to its multi-dimensional challenges, I suggest that the departments target representatives to begin the divisional identification of the issues and needs considered most relevant to determine what formats would be most convenient.

Perhaps the coldest way to assess this sentence would be to ask five impartial readers to describe the author's character. Adjectives like evasive and confused might be used, among others. Simplicity and a direct tone convey intelligence and respect for the reader. Muddy writing conveys just the opposite.

Compare the original sentence with the following revision:

> Each department will send someone to represent it on the committee responsible for developing our final system.

If you received two memos, each containing one version of the sentence, which one would generate a positive response?

CHECK YOURSELF

Rewrite the following sentences to make them clearer.

1. Pursuant to the rules being re-examined as of this date by the administration in charge of Human Resources, endeavour to employ uncomplicated words in writing.

   _____

   _____

2. The occurrence of the accident took place in the area around which we were spending our afternoon in the park closest to the school.

_____

_____

3. What I have done is read every one of the memos in question and pulled out all of the ones that I think we should get the lawyers to look at.

_____

_____

4. Utilization of part-time secretarial personnel will make possible the finalization of the report within the allowable time frame.

_____

_____

5. The expenditure for the purchase of this computer was over £1,000.

_____

_____

6. I made the recommendation that we effect the redistribution of the management of accounts until after our next meeting.

_____

_____

Sample solutions appear at the end of the chapter.

USE THE DIRECT VOICE AND BE BRIEF

Often we use an unnecessarily long or antiquated word when a clear word or short phrase would be better. Here are some simple alternatives to needlessly formal words and phrases:

Instead of	Use
commence	begin
nevertheless	but
terminate	end
advise	tell
despite the fact that	although *or* though
succeed in making	make
give consideration to	consider
have need of	need
we would like to ask that	please

CHECK YOURSELF

Opposite each word or phrase below, write a word or phrase that says the same thing more clearly.

Wordy or complex	Clearer
at the present time	_____
due to the fact that	_____
in order that	_____
with regard to	_____
utilize	_____
visualize	_____
in the near future	_____
ascertain	_____

concur   _____

facilitate   _____

endeavour (as a verb)   _____

in close proximity   _____

in view of the fact that   _____

Sample solutions appear at the end of the chapter.

WRITE IN THE ACTIVE VOICE

The 'active voice' refers to a sentence structure that focuses on a force acting upon an object or situation. 'Passive voice' refers to a sentence structure focusing on an object or situation being acted upon by a force. The following examples demonstrate the difference between the active and passive voice.

Active voice
The manager *restructured* the compensation package and *made* bonuses possible.
The player *scored* a goal.

Passive voice
Bonuses *were made possible* when the compensation package *was restructured* by the manager.
A goal was *scored* by the player.

There are several reasons to choose the active voice. The writer who uses the passive voice may convey a sense of powerlessness. In business writing, the passive voice often appears when morale is low or the writer feels insecure. These negative feelings are conveyed to the readers.

The passive voice also communicates an unwillingness to be direct. 'The reports must be filed by Tuesday' is not as clear as 'You must file the reports by Tuesday'. 'Quarterly goals were not met' does not put the subject in as clear view as 'The sales department did not meet its quarterly goals'. In business writing, the clear view is always the best view.

CHECK YOURSELF

Rewrite these sentences, replacing the passive voice with an active voice. Make the language more direct.

1. The statement of the problem was set forth by the divisional director.

   _____

   _____

2. Avoidance of the problem should be sought.

   _____

   _____

3. It has been suggested that a review board be established by the finance department to oversee cash flow.

   _____

   _____

4. It is believed that an increase in sales over the last quarter would make bonuses a possibility this year.

   _____

   _____

5. Assignments were made without regard for the employee's previous experience and existing responsibilities.

   _____

   _____

Sample solutions appear at the end of the chapter.

USE A TONE THAT CONVEYS CONFIDENCE AND RESPECT

John Vogel, a computer hardware distributor, invited Deirdre Nash, his warehouse manager, into the main office to let off some steam. 'You're holding too much stock on the floor and new orders are accumulating in expensive storage! It's a sign of poor management and I'm not happy with the situation. So do something, fast,' he ordered.

Anxious to show a quick response, Deirdre went back to her desk and reviewed the problem. She found several instances where buyers had not made decisions about how to get equipment delivered or had delivery held up because of payment issues. She fired off several letters, each containing this sentence: 'We cannot hold your equipment any longer than two weeks for any reason, or storage charges will be added to your bill.'

After reading this sentence, customers had several reactions, none of them pleasant: they became nervous, angry or irritated. Customers swamped Deirdre with telephone calls trying to arrange delivery, giving excuses or protesting at the sudden demand that they act. In the end, almost every customer was rattled and unhappy.

A private environmental control agency was given the job of publicizing government standards for acceptable levels of pollutants in waste. The director of the agency, Craig Hastings, wrote to every business and organization that might remotely have been involved in waste disposal. His letters contained this sentence: 'Your company's failure to adhere to government standards for waste disposal will result in significant fines.'

As soon as the letters reached their destinations, Craig started receiving disgruntled calls. 'What makes you think we are polluting?' one caller demanded. 'How dare you threaten us?' said another.

Craig was shocked. 'I was only giving the facts,' he said.

How could Deirdre and Craig have generated support and co-operation rather than anxiety and irritation? Their sentences were grammatically correct and their messages were clear. Still, their letters failed because they did not generate the desired responses.

Put yourself in the position of the person reading Deirdre's letter. If you had read, 'We will be happy to hold your equipment for you for another two weeks without any storage charge and expect that you will be able to arrange its removal by then,' you might have picked up the telephone and asked the distributor to add delivery service to your bill. You probably would not have responded to the letter with a complaint.

If you had read in Craig's letter, 'We have been selected as the local agency responsible for helping you understand government pollution standards and controls,' you probably would not have become defensive and angry. You would have seen Craig as someone helping rather than threatening you. Offers of help typically do not provoke defensive or angry reactions.

Mirroring

If you listen carefully to conversations around you, you will find that negative complaints often receive negative responses; aggressive threats often receive aggressive defences. This pattern is called *mirroring*. You can use this pattern to your advantage because it works as effectively in reverse. Positive tones generally solicit positive responses. Faith and goodwill generate confident co-operation.

Always imagine yourself in the position of the person reading your report, letter or memo. If you seek the reader's respect and competence, make sure you demonstrate respect and competence yourself.

CHECK YOURSELF

Rewrite the following sentences to make them more positive. Use a tone that you want your readers to mirror.

1. If your department continues to fail to meet deadlines, action will be taken.

_____

_____

2. We never take telephone orders on weekends.

_____

_____

3. No one will pay more than £150 for this product.

_____

_____

4. Customer complaints tie us up all day, and normal ongoing work cannot be done.

_____

_____

5. If I had received more timely advice and assistance, the errors would not have been made.

_____

_____

Sample solutions appear at the end of the chapter.

Specificity

Writers must use specific images, situations and data to convey a level of knowledge about any subject. 'I feel that being generous is an important characteristic' doesn't convey as clear a picture of the speaker as 'I give a pound to every homeless person I pass on the street.'

Describing generosity as an important characteristic is vague and theoretical and could have been written by anyone considering the subject. The image of an outstretched hand with a coin shows specific facts and events.

Ask three people from different backgrounds to define the word 'far' and see what happens. To a Londoner, 'far' might be 1 mile. To an Australian it might be 100 miles. To a businessman who travels internationally four times a month, it might be 5,000 miles.

We risk a great deal when we are not specific. We appear to be less informed and we jeopardize the reader's faith in us. When we are not specific, we confuse our readers and often get unexpected or unwanted responses.

Accuracy

Accuracy is critical to gaining our reader's respect and co-operation. If a reader spots one inaccurate fact in a report, he or she will question every other fact in the report. Professional reputations are built by making sure your facts are right. Consistent accuracy inspires trust. It is well worth the time it takes to check facts as well as to edit for style and grammar.

Economy

Rambling or saying more than is necessary gives your reader the impression that you do not know your subject. Saying one word more than you need to is saying too much. Look at the following letter:

---

12 January 1994

Ms Cassandra Smith
Johnson Alarm Company
36 North Crescent
Bath BA5 1HS

Dear Ms Smith,

Last winter we bought some alarms from your company and we've been having trouble with them. As you know, security is an important issue here and walking around feeling that the system doesn't work puts our security people under a constant, irritating strain.

The alarm goes off for no apparent reason and it's reached the point where the staff just ignore it. I don't know if it would work if we actually were burgled because that hasn't happened yet, but it certainly works when we accidentally trip the system on our way to lunch.

If you can't do something about it quickly we will consider going to the local trading standards department to register a complaint.

Yours sincerely,

Harvey Rogers

Consider the questions that Cassandra might ask herself as she read Harvey's letter and tried to respond. Think of her frame of mind and willingness to come to Harvey's aid in the face of a threat to file complaints, particularly when his language implies that she is personally responsible for his problem.

Harvey Rogers has a real problem and a valid complaint. Is he helping Cassandra to solve his problem? What is his invoice identification number, so she can quickly locate an invoice? What kind of alarm system did he purchase? What day was it purchased? When was it installed? Did it come with a warranty?

Two telephone calls, another exchange of letters and three weeks later, Cassandra finally gets enough information to determine what kind of system and warranty Harvey has and how much the repair will cost. Ultimately, Harvey's problem is resolved. Think of the time, energy and aggravation that would have been saved had Harvey been specific and courteous in the first place.

Chapter 5 *Checklist*

✓ When in doubt, use short, to-the-point sentences.
✓ Choose active verbs.
✓ Avoid passive verbs whenever possible.
✓ Let the tone of your message underline your self-confidence.
✓ Ensure that your respect for the reader comes through.
✓ Know your facts before writing.

CHECK YOURSELF SOLUTIONS

Page 61

1. David wants to shorten the time spent managing telemarketers. He also thinks they are not evaluated often enough.
2. I do not believe that the equipment was shipped on time. I also see that the invoicing was not co-ordinated with the ordering process.

Page 62

1. The management would like all employees to write clearly and simply.
2. The accident happened by the park near Hillside School.
3. I have identified the memos that need legal review.
4. Taking on temporary help will make it possible to meet our deadline.

5. The computer cost £1,001.50.
6. I recommend that we redistribute accounts among managers after 31 July.

Page 64

Wordy or complex	Clearer
at the present time	now
due to the fact that	because
in order that	so that
with regard to	as to
utilize	use
visualize	see *or* imagine
in the near future	soon
ascertain	learn *or* understand
concur	agree
facilitate	help *or* make easier
endeavour (as a verb)	try
in close proximity	near
in view of the fact that	because of *or* due to

Page 66

1. The divisional director stated the problem.
2. We should avoid the problem.
3. We suggest that the finance department forms a review board to oversee cash flow.
4. Increased sales over the last quarter will make bonuses a possibility this year.
5. He (or she) assigned positions without regard for previous experience and existing responsibilities.

Page 68

1. If your department meets deadlines, it will be regarded as highly successful.
2. We take telephone orders from Monday to Friday, from 8 A.M. to 6 P.M.
3. People will pay as much as £150 for this product.
4. A great deal of our work is responding to customer complaints.
5. Timely advice and assistance can prevent errors from happening.

CHAPTER 6

Paragraphs That Work

> **This chapter will help you to:**
> - **keep paragraphs unified**
> - **control paragraph length**
> - **position a topic sentence effectively**
> - **build transitions between paragraphs**

Paragraphs make your thoughts more accessible to readers. They break your entire document – whether it be a letter, memo, report, or proposal – into blocks of related sentences. This makes it easier for you and your reader to predict what's coming, to find what you're looking for and to get the main points by skimming.

WHAT IS A PARAGRAPH?

A paragraph is a group of sentences related to one another by a single idea or subject. Just as every word in a sentence must be necessary, so every sentence in a paragraph must serve a purpose.

A simple rule about paragraphs is: one paragraph, one idea. The most common mistake writers make is putting too much into one paragraph.

Paragraphs organize materials and control the visual impact of the page. Pages of text with no breaks or white space tire the reader's eye. Breaking the same words into tightly conceived paragraphs will create a more inviting page that is easier to understand.

Look at the letters on the next two pages.

Physical Theatre Company
One Park Square
Cambridge CB1 5SJ

13 June 1993

Paula Anderson, Dance Co-ordinator
National Foundation for the Arts
2 Brayburn Avenue
London SW1 4FV

Dear Paula,

We write to notify you of a change in plans for one of the key players in the Physical Theatre Company's programme which you funded this year. Last year, when we were putting together our programme for 1994–95, we asked John Ellery to choreograph a new dance specially for our company. When he said yes, we proceeded to draft a proposal to the National Foundation, asking for financial support for that project. Upon hearing of our award, we contacted Johnny to confirm dates for his first visit. We then learned that he is no longer available to set the work. His manager has arranged a very lucrative tour for him in the US, so he is unavailable until 1995. We now have the choice of waiting for his return or finding a new choreographer. We feel that the company needs a new dance for its forthcoming season, and we believe that a work by Elaine Massey would meet our artistic needs as well as one by Johnny. We are writing to ask if we can simply use the funds you awarded us for Johnny's work and apply them to another dance. We believe that the award was made in the spirit of extending the Physical Theatre Company's repertoire rather than furthering Johnny's career, so you will not mind the switch. As you know, the £15,000 award included travel and accommodation for him and two members of his company five times during the period he worked with us, and a fee for permanent rights to the dance. It also included the standard costs of costume designers, lighting designers, our own dancers' time, an accompanist, and production costs for its first performance. We have discussed the particulars of the budget with Elaine and she feels she could contain costs to match the existing budget, so no new funds would be needed. We appreciate the NFA's flexibility and commitment to the development of individual dance company repertoires, and hope you will agree to this change. A reply before the end of July would make it possible for Elaine to make the necessary changes to her schedule. Thank you for your time and attention.

Yours sincerely,

Peter O'Connor
General Manager, Physical Theatre Company

Physical Theatre Company
One Park Square
Cambridge CB1 5SJ

13 June 1993

Paula Anderson, Dance Co-ordinator
National Foundation for the Arts
2 Brayburn Avenue
London SW1 4FV

Dear Paula,

We write to notify you of a change in plans for one of the key players in the Physical Theatre Company's programme which you funded this year.

Last year, when we were putting together our programme for 1994–95, we asked John Ellery to choreograph a new dance specifically for our company. When he said yes, we proceeded to draft a proposal to the National Foundation, asking for financial support for that project. Upon hearing of our award, we contacted Johnny to confirm dates for his first visit. We then learned that he is no longer available to set the work. His manager has arranged a very lucrative tour for him in the US, so he is unavailable until 1995.

We now have the choice of waiting for his return or finding a new choreographer. The company needs a new dance for its forthcoming season, and we believe that a work by Elaine Massey would meet our artistic needs as well as one by Johnny.

We are writing to ask if we can simply use the funds you awarded us for Johnny's work and apply them to another dance.

We believe that the award was made in the spirit of extending the Physical Theatre Company's repertoire rather than furthering Johnny's career, so you will not mind the switch.

We have discussed the particulars of the budget with Elaine and she feels she could contain costs to match the existing budget, so no new funds would be needed.

We appreciate the NFA's flexibility and commitment to the development of individual dance company repertoires, and hope you will agree to this change.

A reply before the end of July would enable Elaine to make the necessary changes to her schedule. Thank you for your time and attention.

Yours sincerely,

Peter O'Connor
General Manager, Physical Theatre Company

The two letters convey virtually the same information, although the second one contains fewer sentences. Which letter do you think communicates more clearly?

THE TOPIC SENTENCE

In a paragraph, the topic sentence presents the main idea.

Every sentence in the following paragraph supports the statement made in the topic sentence (in bold type).

> **Finally, after two years of effort, I fulfilled my dream of seeing the lake at sunset.** This was harder to accomplish than you might think because sunset is the time of day when my children are most demanding. After months of painting glorious pictures of all the amusements found on lakes at sunset, I convinced my children to co-operate. I got my wish and drove off at last, hoping their good humour would last through the adventure.

Topic sentences do not have to appear at the beginning of a paragraph, though readers typically look for them there. Here is an example of how the paragraph above could be restructured to shift the topic sentence's position:

> My children resisted me right down the line. I struggled to move them, but late afternoon was their most demanding and least co-operative time of day. For months I painted glorious pictures of all the amusements found on the lake at sunset and at long last my children got in the car and promised to humour me. **Finally, after two years of effort, I fulfilled my dream of seeing the lake at sunset.**

Think of paragraphs as having shapes, with the topic sentence appearing at the most focused part.

Common Paragraph Designs

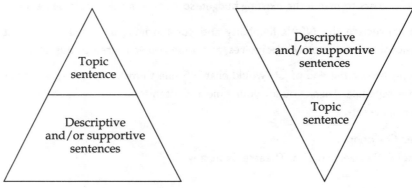

CHECK YOURSELF

Below you will find four paragraphs. Underline the topic sentence of each one.

1. All the frustrations of Andy's day left him feeling short-tempered and anxious. The moment he arrived at work, he discovered three errors in the night shift's work. Worse, the errors attracted a great deal of attention because Andy's own boss chose this particular day to drop in and review the morning shipping schedule. Not only did everything seem to go wrong, but everyone in the world seemed to be watching it happen.

2. The best way to handle paperwork is to touch each document that crosses your desk only once. If a document is highly important, telephone, write or dictate a response immediately. If it is moderately important, dash off a reply directly on the letter or memo itself, or redirect it to an appropriate person. If you believe it could wait, let it wait – forever. Toss it in a special drawer that holds things you never expect to do. This is the most efficient use of your time.

3. You can be someone who works methodically, never leaving any detail to rest until your work seems perfect. You can be sweepingly quick, happier accomplishing a great deal than one perfect thing. You can be a dreamer who is concerned with nothing at all but what is in your head at any given moment. You can succeed no matter what kind of person you are, if only you find a life's work that fits your character.

4. People typically do not think of prejudice in the workplace as something that extends to those with weight problems, but it does. We know that women, the disabled and ethnic minorities suffer job discrimination. It is also true that individuals who are more than 20 pounds overweight are offered less money to do the same job as slender colleagues; in some cases the overweight are even rejected for jobs for no reason other than their physical appearance.

The solutions appear at the end of the chapter.

LENGTH

Paragraphs can be 2 or 3 or 20 sentences long. In business writing, try to keep them brief. Short paragraphs make documents look accessible and well-organized. They make it possible to scan an entire document quickly and find the information you need.

When choosing between a shorter and a longer paragraph, choose the shorter one. Don't be afraid of white space on the page.

TRANSITIONS

All the paragraphs in a letter, memo or report must be linked together like rungs on a ladder. Sentences that connect paragraphs are called *transitions*. They give shape and direction to letters, memos and reports.

The following example shows transition sentences that could begin each of the paragraphs of a letter requesting a company to re-examine its leave policies.

> The first paragraph asks the company to consider dividing a management job into two part-time positions.

Transition sentence to second paragraph: Consider these three reasons for this kind of job reconstruction.

> The second paragraph offers one good reason for considering this kind of job reconstruction, citing a research study which indicates that part-time people working half-time accomplish 89 per cent of what full-timers accomplish. The paragraph goes on to offer examples supporting the research findings.

Transition sentence to third paragraph: Besides productivity, employee levels of job satisfaction were higher.

> The third paragraph describes how job satisfaction positively influences the quality of people's work.

Transition sentence to fourth paragraph: Another result of job satisfaction is improved attendance.

> The fourth paragraph describes a study of hundreds of employees who evaluated their level of job satisfaction. Low satisfaction correlated significantly with higher absenteeism and lateness.

Transition sentence to concluding paragraph: Ultimately, splitting professional jobs makes sense.

> The concluding paragraph wraps up the argument that restructuring professional jobs into part-time positions can improve productivity, work quality and attendance rates.

Many words and phrases help make transitions smooth. Most are phrases that point the reader forward to the next idea.

Common transitional words and phrases

similarly	in the meantime
beyond	after a while
meanwhile	on the contrary
ultimately	in contrast to
subsequently	at the same time
therefore	equally important
finally	in addition
moreover	in the future
also	to sum up
first	on the whole
second	in other words
third	for example

CHECK YOURSELF

Insert appropriate transitional words or phrases in the blanks that follow.

1. _____ part-time workers are typically more productive per hour than their full-time colleagues, most employers are reluctant to hire part-time staff.

2. _____, many employers limit career advancement for the few who manage to negotiate part-time contracts. There are several reasons why this attitude damages companies.

3. _____, it is better to have several people under your roof who know a job rather than just one, who might leave and take away important information that no one else has.

4. _____, part-timers are usually willing to negotiate minimal or reasonable benefits packages.

5. _____ full-timers whose benefits can total over 35 per cent of their salaries.

6. _____, part-timers often repay a flexible employer with unusually high morale and hard work.

7. Full-timers, _____, often get burned out by the relentless demands of jobs that do not accommodate family or educational demands.

8. _____, employers could gain great benefits by experimenting more with job-sharing and new work schedule arrangements.

A sample solution appears at the end of the chapter.

Chapter 6 *Checklist*

✓ One idea = one paragraph.
✓ Link paragraphs with clear transition sentences.
✓ Become familiar with good transition phrases.
✓ Hone your topic sentences to:
    give shape and focus to your paragraphs;
    capture the reader's attention;
    give yourself a starting-point.
✓ Avoid one-sentence paragraphs, but keep them brief.

CHECK YOURSELF SOLUTIONS

Page 77

1. <u>All the frustrations of Andy's day left him feeling short-tempered and anxious</u>. The moment he arrived at work, he discovered three errors in the night shift's work. Worse, the errors attracted a great deal of attention because Andy's own boss chose this particular day to drop in and review the morning shipping schedule. Not only did everything seem to go wrong, but everyone in the world seemed to be watching it happen.

2. <u>The best way to handle paperwork is to touch each document that crosses your desk only once.</u> If a document is highly important, telephone, write or dictate a response immediately. If it is moderately important, dash off a reply directly on the letter or memo itself, or redirect it to an appropriate person. If you believe it could wait, let it wait – forever. Toss it in a special drawer that holds things you never expect to do. This is the most efficient use of your time.

3. You can be someone who works methodically, never leaving any detail to rest until your work seems perfect. You can be sweepingly quick, happier accomplishing a great deal than one perfect thing. You can be a dreamer who is concerned with nothing at all but what is in your head at any given moment. <u>You can succeed no matter what kind of person you are, if only you find a life's work that fits your character.</u>

4. <u>People typically do not think of prejudice in the workplace as something that extends to those with weight problems, but it does.</u> We know that women, the disabled and ethnic minorities suffer job discrimination. But it is also true that individuals who are more than 20 pounds overweight are offered less money to do the same job as slender colleagues; in some cases the overweight are even rejected for jobs for no reason other than their physical appearance.

Page 79

1. Although
2. Moreover
3. First
4. Second

5. in contrast to
6. Third *or* Finally
7. on the other hand *or* however
8. To sum up *or* In conclusion

CHAPTER 7

Write for Results

> This chapter will help you to:
> - recognize common writing practices that diminish the effect of your correspondence
> - prepare superior letters and memos through applying principles to write for results

Charlotte Cox, a solicitor's clerk, took time one day to re-read some letters she had written. To her dismay, she found she had fallen into some poor writing habits. She wrote wordy sentences, used jargon frequently and talked down to the clients. She recognized sentences that would have been more emphatic with the simple use of an active verb. She knew that she needed to brush up her writing skills.

Chapter 7 is designed to help experienced writers like Charlotte, as well as novice writers, recognize when to use the write-for-results principles.

USE AS FEW WORDS AS POSSIBLE

A recent graduate began his CV with the following career objective:

OBJECTIVE

To be in a position to utilize my excellent preparation, my meaningful work experience and my outstanding people skills in a middle management position that will give me a good opportunity to grow professionally and personally in very important ways.

Does this statement impress you? Probably not. Would you think 'Just tell me what your objective is!' The fewer words you use, the more powerful your message is.

Excessive words can easily creep into your writing. Check the list on the left below. Do any of these appear in your writing?

Excessive wording	Improved wording	
at a later date	later *or* then	_____
at all times	always	
at this point in time	now	_____
can be in a position to	can	
due to the fact that	because	_____
each and every one	every one	
firstly, secondly, thirdly	first, second, third	_____
in compliance with your request	at your request	
in the event of	if	_____
in the majority of instances	usually	
inasmuch as	since	_____
on a monthly basis	monthly	
owing to the fact that	since	_____

Can you think of wordy expressions you use? Add them to the list above.

NEVER USE TWO WORDS WHEN ONE WILL DO

Most of us say more than is necessary to make our point. We carry this habit over into our writing. Redundant expressions are another form of excessive wording. Some have become such clichés that you may not even recognize them as redundant.

Can you identify the redundancies in the following sentence?

The consensus of opinion is that our advance planning was absolutely essential.

Did you spot consensus *of opinion, advance* planning, *absolutely* essential? Look at the following list of other common redundant expressions. Note that each of the italicized words is unnecessary.

actual experience	*final* conclusion
and *etc.*	first *and foremost*
ask *the question*	following *after*
attached *hereto*	for *a period of* two weeks
at some later *date*	*foreign* imports
basic fundamentals	*free* gratis
blend/join/merge/mix *together*	goals *and objectives*
circle *around*	*group* meeting

close proximity/scrutiny	large/small *in size*
collect/combine *together*	*mutual* co-operation
completely filled	*new* innovation
consequent results	*one and* the same
continue *on*	*past* experience
co-operate *together*	plan *ahead/for the future/in advance*
disappear *from sight*	reason *is because*
enclosed *herewith*	recur/repeat *again*
estimated *to be about*	same *identical*
exact opposites	*true* facts
few *in number*	

Underline any of the above expressions that you use. This will increase your awareness of the phrase and help you eliminate it from your writing.

USE POSITIVE WORDS AND PHRASES

There was a popular song in the 1940s called 'Accentuate the Positive!' Perhaps the composer was also a writer of business letters because the advice is excellent. Compare the two sentences below.

Negative statement
You overlooked the fact that you failed to make last month's payment.
Positive statement
Were you aware that you did not send last month's payment?

Which statement is more likely to elicit a positive response from the customer? Which one would you respond to?

Negative expressions can be either direct or implied. If a sentence reads, 'You are not qualified for the position', it is a direct negative. If the same sentence reads, 'You need more experience to qualify for this position', it is negative by implication. Your task as a writer is to convey negative information in positive language.

Remember, your ultimate goal is to bring about a positive response or action from the reader. You accomplish this more quickly if you do not scold or make the reader feel guilty.

Two pointers may help you create positive statements for negative situations.

- Avoid beginning a sentence with *you*. You will find that you write a softer sentence when the *you* is placed within the sentence. *Did you understand my point?* is much softer than *You failed to understand my point.*
- Substitute *when* for *if*. *When you complete your work, we will process your salary increase* implies confidence in the reader more than *If you complete your work, we will process your salary increase.*

AVOID CLICHÉS AND USE JARGON ONLY WHEN APPROPRIATE

Clichés are fad phrases and trite expressions. Initially these can be very effective, but with overuse they quickly lose their punch. An example is *user-friendly*, a term that became popular in the early 1980s along with personal computers. It has long since lost its impact.

Many business writers use far too many trite phrases. Your letters and memos should represent your personal expression rather than stilted tradition. Give your correspondence a fresh face; aim for a warm, conversational tone.

There are thousands of clichés in our language. A few of the familiar ones in business usage are listed here. Be aware of clichés in your own writing and eliminate them.

ballpark figure	input
bottom line	maximize
cost-effective	prioritize
dialogue	state of the art
enclosed herewith	take on board
first and foremost	thank you in advance
hands on	

Jargon is insider talk – words and phrases understood by people in a particular profession or industry. Jargon is a necessary part of communication between persons in the profession but is inappropriate when writing to those outside your industry who may be unfamiliar with them. As we saw in Chapter 1, jargon interferes with clarity. Samples of jargon taken from several professions would include:

cash cow	feasibility study
VDU	interface
debug	needs assessment
DTP	normative sample
extended family	quality cycles
facilitator	

As you identify jargon in your communications, be sure you observe the following guidelines:

- Limit its use to those readers who understand it.
- If you must use jargon, include its meaning the first time you use it.

BE AWARE OF SEXISM

Good businesss writers are careful to eliminate all sexist language or assumptions from their writing. In the past, sexism has been evident in two forms:

The use of sexist designations: postman or stewardess.

The use of sexist pronoun references: the doctor and *his* patients, the nurse and *her* patients.

Sexism in writing can be eliminated in three ways:

- Using *his/her* in place of a single *his* or *her*:

  Each employee must prepare his/her own report.

  Note: Many writers consider this an awkward construction and avoid it whenever possible.

- Changing the noun to a plural form and using *their*:

  All employees must prepare their own reports.

- Rewriting the sentence to avoid the use of a pronoun:

  Reports must be prepared by individual students.

Eliminating sexism from your writing does not mean that you accept a certain political system or philosophy. It simply means that you acknowledge the equality of roles that exist in business today. The following are samples of gender-specific terms that have changed in recent years.

Original phrase	Improved phrase
fireman	firefighter
headmistress	headteacher
man hours	working hours
policeman	police officer
salesman	salesperson

CHECK YOURSELF

Apply the five write-for-results principles you have just reviewed by rewriting the following sentences.

Using as few words as possible

Pursuant to your personal letter of 15 May 1995, we wish to inform you that the aggregate amount of your purchase leaves an account balance of £259.95.

_____

_____

_____

Eliminating redundant expressions

It is my personal opinion that the statement attached hereto contains the true facts in the case.

_____

_____

_____

Using positive words and phrases

If you will take time to read the enclosed brochure, you will understand why we demand prompt payment of all accounts.

_____

_____

_____

Eliminating clichés and jargon

Thank you in advance for helping us prioritize our needs.

_____

_____

_____

Avoiding sexist references

The future of each employee lies in his own hands.

_____

_____

_____

Sample solutions are at the end of the chapter.

USE THE ACTIVE VOICE

Perhaps you will remember the classic definition: active verbs act; passive verbs are acted upon.

Active verb: Our York branch _tests_ all new products.
Passive verb: All new products _are tested_ at our York branch.

Using active verbs adds power to your writing. Active verbs are more dynamic than passive verbs. Active verbs move your reader to action. Active verbs result in shorter sentences.

Passive verbs can be identified by the presence of an auxiliary or linking verb (is, are, am, was, or were). Compare the two forms below.

Active verb	Passive verb
communicates	are communicated
analysed	were analysed
thought	was thought

Passive verbs in sentences can usually be converted to active ones by rewriting the sentence. When you rewrite, be careful that you do not change the meaning.

Passive: The new policy was recommended by Gerard.
Active: Gerard recommended the new policy.

Passive: It has been decided to cancel the programme.
Active: The Executive Committee cancelled the programme.

Use the passive voice when the subject of the sentence or the doer of the action is more important than the action.

Appropriate use of passive voice
Minimum standards will be established for all new employees.
(The standards are more important than the employees.)

The worker was seriously injured by the falling beam.
(The worker is more important than the beam.)

WRITE *TO* AND NOT *DOWN TO* YOUR READER

The use of condescending words and phrases in your writing is a more abstract concept than some of the writing principles discussed previously. Condescending expressions are a matter of tone rather than specific words. The same words can be acceptable in one situation and unacceptable in another. Condescending is talking down to the reader, who senses a scolding or 'I told you so' attitude.

A condescending tone is most apt to creep into your writing when you are displeased with the reader or with the reader's action or lack of action.

Condescending: As you are well aware, our policy is to satisfy our customers.
Improved: As a valued customer, your satisfaction is our goal.

Notice that the first sentence is me-oriented and thus condescending. The second sentence is you-oriented. Which one evokes a positive response from you?

Unfortunately, some writers use a condescending tone to boost their own egos or to express their own sense of self-importance. A common way of doing this is through the use of jargon.

Condescending: The documentation for your LAN will answer all your questions. If you don't understand the instructions, ring our technical support system.
Improved: You will find the manual for your network very helpful. If you have additional questions, our support staff on 0800-225-8989 are eager to help you.

If you had recently installed a computer network, which sentence would you respond to?

Keep calm

Every business writer has moments of anger or exasperation. If you can, avoid writing during those times. If you must write, put the letter or memo aside. Read it later and alter the tone before sending it.

LONG WORDS ARE UNNECESSARY

Do you want to write power-packed messages? Use short, plain words. Too often the only person you impress with long words is yourself.

Your writing should be appropriate for your audience. Think of the people you most often write to: customers, clients and colleagues. All these people would rather do business with a warm, helpful human being than a cold, robotlike individual.

What about your superiors? Many executives will tell you that they respond to clear, plain, short messages. They do not have time to interpret your impressive use of the language.

Stilted language: The cessation of the policy will occur at 12:01 A.M. 15 July.

Improved language: The policy expires at 12:01 A.M. 15 July.

Too many long words: You should proceed to investigate the findings of the study.

Improved language: Continue your study of the findings.

How can you develop the good writing habit of using simple language?

- Write the message naturally, including any long words that come to you.
- Reread the message. Did you write to impress rather than to express?
- Ask yourself: What am I really trying to say?
- Rewrite the message.
- Write down any long words you use unnecessarily. Remember, awareness is the first step to improvement.

Keep it simple

Have you ever heard a reader complain that a letter or memo was too easy to understand?

CHECK YOURSELF

The three writing principles you have just reviewed focused on enhancing your writing skills. Let's apply this skill to some sample sentences. Rewrite the following sentences to illustrate:

Using active verbs

The new holiday policy was approved by the staff and will give employees with five years or more service an added week of holiday.

_____

_____

Avoiding a condescending tone

Since we have done business for many years, you should know that we require payment upon delivery, unless prior arrangements have been made.

_____

_____

Using simple words

Enclosed herewith is a copy of the recently passed legislation empowering home-owners to appeal against the tax bands established for their properties.

_____

_____

Suggested sample solutions are at the end of the chapter.

WRITE DIRECTLY TO THE INTERESTS OF THE READER

Not considering the interests of your reader could be the reason for other writing problems. If you consciously consider the interests of your reader, you are likely to observe good writing principles. How can you do this?

Visualize your reader. Imagine that you and your reader are in the same room holding a conversation. What level of language would you use? What tone would you use to maintain a positive discussion? What information would you give that person? What response would you expect? All these questions represent issues you want to keep in mind when writing, guaranteeing that you think of your reader first.

Business writing books have called this approach the 'you attitude'. It emphasizes *you* instead of *I/we/me/us*. Consider the following sentences:

I/me attitude	You attitude
If we do not receive your cheque immediately, we will be unable to continue shipping your orders without pre-payment.	You have always enjoyed priority shipping status. You can retain this convenient rating by sending us your cheque immediately.

While I remember with pleasure my appearance last year at your awards banquet, I am not available on 30 July this year to speak to your group.

What a pleasure it was to speak to your group last year. I sincerely wish I could join you again this year but, unfortunately, I have another engagement.

How would you feel?

When you are the reader, what writing tone elicits a favourable response? In other words, if you were the reader, how would you react to the letter you've just written?

ARE THE DETAILS CORRECT?

Do you think your job is done when you finish writing a letter? Composing the letter is only the first step.

As the writer, you are also responsible for error-free copy, accurate information or details and appropriate formatting. If you send your letters to an assistant for typing, you hope that person will also assume some responsibility for the accuracy of the contents. However, when you sign the letter, you are implying approval of the contents and the appearance. Do you take pride in the letters bearing your signature? Are you reasonably certain of their accuracy?

The quality of your correspondence is a reflection of you. What image are you projecting?

- Scan your correspondence before signing it. Does it appear balanced on the page? Is there enough white space to encourage reading?
- Read the letter for content. Does it say what you intend to say? Is the tone positive?
- Read the letter for accuracy. Are the spelling and grammar correct? Are names, dates and other details correct?

CHECK YOURSELF

You have just completed the review of the final two write-for-results principles: considering the interests of the reader and paying attention to details. Both of these represent important refinements in your writing.

Read the sentences below. Write an improved version of each one.

Considering the interests of the reader

We are unable to fill your order for one filing cabinet because you failed to specify the colour or size.

_____

_____

Paying attention to details

Each of the divisions have made a firm commitment to better quality control.

_____

_____

_____

Sample solutions are at the end of the chapter.

PUTTING IT ALL TOGETHER

Now that you are aware of the ten write-for-results principles of business writing, you are ready to apply them in your writing.

CHAPTER 7 *Checklist*

✓ Write brief sentences.
✓ Use simple words.
✓ Make a positive approach.
✓ Avoid jargon.
✓ Use non-sexist language.
✓ Have a friendly tone.
✓ Use the active voice.
✓ Write to and for the reader.
✓ Pay attention to details.
✓ Keep it clear.

CHECK YOURSELF SOLUTIONS

Page 87

Using as few words as possible
The current balance on your account is £259.95.

Eliminating redundant expressions
In my opinion, the attached statement contains the facts in the case.

Using positive words and phrases
The enclosed brochure will help you understand why prompt payments are important.

Eliminating clichés and jargon
Thank you for helping us set our priorities.

Avoiding sexist references
Employees hold their future within their own hands.

Page 91

Using active verbs
The new holiday policy, approved by the staff, gives employees with five or more years of service one additional week's holiday.

Avoiding a condescending tone
We continue to maintain our policy of payment due upon delivery, unless prior arrangements have been made.

Using simple words
Enclosed is a copy of a leaflet which explains to home-owners their right to appeal against council tax bands.

Page 94

Considering the interests of the reader
Please indicate on the enclosed postcard the colour and size of the filing cabinet you wish to order, and we will process your order immediately.

Paying attention to details
Each of the divisions has made a firm commitment to better quality control.

CHAPTER 8

Inter-Office Memos

This chapter will help you to:
- **develop your memo image**
- **write memos with a purpose**
- **master the principles of successful memo writing**
- **send effective electronic messages**

Curtis Owen, office manager of Superior Office Products, writes several memos every day. In fact, since his responsibilities are internal, he seldom writes a letter.

Recently he distributed a memo that contained some very important information. Later he overheard two of his employees talking: 'Doesn't Curtis have anything else to do but write memos? They are always so long!' The second employee replied, 'I've learned to glance at the subject line; if I think it's a "must read", I do. Otherwise, it goes in my "do later" pile. Someone should just tell him that enough is enough!'

This scene is repeated in too many offices every day. Are your memos taken seriously? Chapter 8 will help you take a critical look at your memo-writing practices and provide you with guidelines to increase the acceptability of your memos.

MEMOS, MEMOS, MEMOS!

Do you find that you read and write more memos than letters? If so, you are typical of today's business writer.

Do you feel confident that you can write a memo that commands attention and gets results? Since memos represent internal communication, they tend to accumulate in other people's files, including those of your superiors. What is the memo image of your file?

Is your image fresh? Does a glance at your memos invite reading? Does the content of your memos convey conciseness, preciseness, inclusiveness and warmth? Or are your memos dull? Are they wordy, vague, stilted and even unnecessary?

Formatting the memo

Your memo image begins with the appearance of the memo. Apply these checkpoints to the sample memo below.

- Is it one page in length?
- Are related items aligned?
- Are the paragraphs short?
- If you scan the memo, does it look readable – and thus invite reading?
- When appropriate, have you used a list format rather than a narrative?
- Does it contain as much white space as possible?

MEMORANDUM

TO: Edward Simons
FROM: Anan Singh
DATE: 9 August 199–
SUBJECT: INDUSTRIAL SOCIETY MEETING

Thank you so much for agreeing to speak to the Industrial Society's meeting on 15 October 199—. I am sure you will find this an enjoyable occasion.

The details are: Industrial Society
Admiral Hotel – Marina Room
15 October 199–
12 noon lunch
20-minute talk on a topic of your choice.

Your contact person, Joyce Roberts, will ring you within the next few days.

jjk

Did you notice that you can answer each of these checkpoints simply by scanning the memo, without having to read it?

Inter-office memos may be printed on plain paper or printed forms. In either case, four items always appear:

- the name of the addressee(s)
- the name of the originator

- the date the memo is written
- the subject of the memo

Checklist for memo details

- When a memo is being sent to several people, replace individual names with a *distribution list*.
- Usually place the names in a distribution list in alphabetical order. You may place names in order of seniority or rank within the organization. Caution: A ranked list opens the possibility of misplacing a name.
- Do not use job titles in memos.
- Use a descriptive subject line.
- Replace the signature line by the handwritten initials of the originator at the top of the memo.

PREPARING TO WRITE THE MEMO

Effective writing always begins with planning. Planning begins when you answer one critical question:

What do I want the reader to know or do after reading this memo?

Once you have decided what you want the reader to know or do, you are ready to plan the memo. Planning is a three-step process:

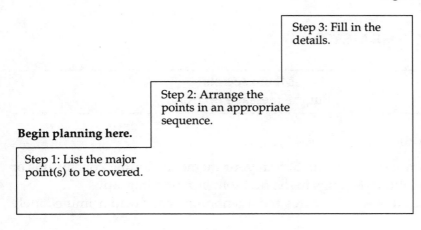

Begin writing here.

Step 3: Fill in the details.

Step 2: Arrange the points in an appropriate sequence.

Begin planning here.

Step 1: List the major point(s) to be covered.

CHECK YOURSELF

Kaye Watt, office manager for Southwest Products, must write a memo to initiate the following three changes in procedures. Parcels to be sent by a private carrier must be received by 3.30 P.M. First-class post must be received by 4.00 P.M. All post must be received in the post room by 4.30 P.M. to be sent out the same day. These changes are to take effect from 15 July.

Step 1: List the major points to be covered. (Four lines are provided; you may have fewer or more points.)

_____

_____

_____

_____

Step 2: Number the points you listed above in the desired sequence by writing 1, 2, 3 or 4 in the space to the left of each line.

Step 3: Since this is an exercise, you will skip Step 3 – filling in the details . In actual practice, always complete this step before you begin to write.

A sample solution appears at the end of the chapter.

WRITING THE MEMO

```
                          Memo secrets
                     Put the message up front.
```

The opening

The most important information in your memo, including conclusions or recommendations, belongs in the first sentence or paragraph.

Writing in this way captures the attention of your reader immediately and makes your reason for writing clear. It sets the stage for action or decisions.

Read the following opening paragraph:

> Sometimes big corporations are accused of being indifferent to human needs. I think that is why I was so pleased to learn of a recent series of events that involved a group of our employees in the Derby plant.

What important information is conveyed in this paragraph? Does it really grab your interest? Or, do you respond in a 'Ho hum, that's nice' manner? How would you respond to the paragraph below if you received this memo in the middle of a hectic day in which everything had gone wrong?

> Twenty-three maintenance technicians in our Derby plant are each giving £1 a week to support a new day centre for the elderly in Matlock – an impressive display of teamwork and generosity.

Would you agree that this opening paragraph is more intriguing, leading you to continue reading? The main point is in the first paragraph.

Memo secrets
Say only what is necessary.

The main message

The succeeding paragraphs of your memo briefly support the important information already conveyed in the first paragraph. Only relevant information is included. Nice-to-know information does not have a place in memos.

Listings may be used very effectively with some types of information. Consider the following main message paragraph of a memo:

> You might wish to consider the following topics as you plan your presentation: Quality Circles, Management with Meaning, The Corporate Ladder Has a Missing Rung, or High Tech – Low Performance. I think any of these would be well received.

compared to:

Possible topics include:
- Quality Circles
- Management with Meaning
- The Corporate Ladder Has a Missing Rung
- High Tech – Low Performance

Notice how much more readable the second example is? Even a quick read conveys the message.

Memo secrets
Eliminate unnecessary closing remarks.

The closing

Unlike business letters, the best memo closing may be none. Use a closing only when you need to convey a final item of information.

Look at the following closing paragraph of a memo.

When you have had an opportunity to consider all the options, please give me a ring. If you have any questions, please do not hesitate to contact me.

This closing contains no necessary information. It is weakened even more by the vague reference, *please give me a call*. It continues its ineffectiveness by ending with a cliché: *if you have any questions, please do not hesitate to contact me.*

Can this closing be improved? No. It is unnecessary and therefore should not even be written.

Please meet in my office on Tuesday 3 August at 9.00 A.M. to finalize these plans.

This is an example of a closing paragraph that is effective – written in brief, specific language.

PUTTING IT ALL TOGETHER

Writing is easy . . . when you remember:
Determining your purpose for writing **precedes** preparing a writing plan, which **precedes** writing a first draft, which **precedes** writing a final copy.

CHECK YOURSELF

Now that you have reviewed the basic principles of planning and writing memos, it is time to put your new skill to work. Refer to the preceding pages as often as necessary.

First, prepare a memo plan for the situation described below. Then, write a first draft of the memo. Finally, do any necessary rewriting or editing for a final copy.

> Write a memo to all department managers telling them that the preliminary architectural plans for a building extension are ready to be reviewed. These plans will be presented by Len Victor, the managing director of your company, at a meeting on Tuesday of next week in your office. Each manager should bring 12 copies of the respective five-year department plans. This is an exciting meeting because these plans have been in the works for 36 months.

A sample solution appears at the end of the chapter. Look at the important points in the suggested memo and compare them with those in your memo.

THE ELECTRONIC MESSAGE – AN INSTANT MEMO

The use of electronic messages is growing rapidly. What do you need to know to use this medium successfully?

Electronic messages are another form of inter-office memo. Many of the checkpoints from the previous chapter also apply to electronic messages. In addition, the following guidelines will be helpful to you.

Effective electronic messages

- The reader cannot see your face; thus, the nuances of communication are missing. Avoid jokes, sarcasm, threats or any tools of verbal communication that might be misinterpreted.
- Write an attention-getting opening sentence. As more and more messages are sent, yours must stand out if it is to be read.
- Write the main message – and the main message only.
- Limit your message to one screen, if possible.

- Review your message before sending it. Is it grammatically correct? Are all words spelled correctly? Your image and your credibility are on the line.
- Avoid using the system for personal messages. Electronic messages may not be as private as you think.
- Be sure you save or print a copy when you need a record of your message.

Electronic message secrets
Remember there is a human being at the other end of the line.

Chapter 8 *Checklist*

Memo-writing

✓ Always begin with a writing plan.
✓ Put the most important information in the first sentence or paragraph.
✓ Tell the reader what you want done as quickly as possible.
✓ Write short, simple sentences.
✓ When appropriate, use a listing to expand or support the main message.
✓ Eliminate all unnecessary information.
✓ Eliminate unnecessary closing remarks.

Memo protocol

✓ Never write a memo you are unwilling to have other people read.
✓ Never assume that memo information will be kept confidential.
✓ Never ignore the chain of command.
✓ Avoid exaggeration.
✓ Avoid humour; never use sarcasm.
✓ Don't use a memo to criticize another person or department.
✓ If you write a negative memo, delay sending it.

CHECK YOURSELF SOLUTIONS

Page 100

Step 1. The three new post and parcel deadlines.
Step 2. Effective date.

Page 103

Memo plan

1. Details of presentation
2. Reminder to bring 12 copies of five-year department plans.

Suggested memo

The preliminary architectural plans for our extension will be presented by Len Victor on Tuesday 15 March at 9 A.M. in my office. Please bring 12 copies of your five-year department plans for distribution.

CHAPTER 9

Letters

This chapter will help you to:
- **understand why you write letters**
- **plan your writing for success**
- **write each part of the letter to achieve the desired result**
- **format correspondence to project a contemporary image**

Charles Jones is a very careful writer. He puts considerable time and effort into the many letters he writes during a normal business day. However, he often feels frustrated because his readers either do not respond or ring up for additional information. Sometimes he wonders why he works so hard at writing. He suspects that much of his correspondence is not even read.

If this sounds familiar, then Chapter 9 is written just for you.

WHY DO YOU WRITE LETTERS?

Have you ever asked yourself why you write letters? Perhaps you think that is a foolish question. The truth is, most of us write without ever asking this critical question. Perhaps we don't ask the question because the answer is obvious: we write to get results.

The next question is, how often do your letters bring the desired results? Almost always, usually, or less often than you wish? What are the secrets of successful business letters – letters that get results?

FOUR CRITICAL QUESTIONS

You can write letters that bring results if you answer four questions before you begin to write.

Why am I writing?

What is your reason for writing? The majority of business letters are written for one of the following purposes:

- to invite or respond
- to enquire or request
- to express appreciation or regret
- to remind
- to move to action

If you cannot identify a specific purpose for writing, perhaps you don't need to write a letter. A phone call or a visit might achieve your goals.

To whom am I writing?

What do you know about your reader? When you know the personality of your reader, you have the advantage of tailoring your letter. When you don't know your reader, or when your reader is part of a generic group (i.e., clients or customers), you must write your letters to communicate a warm human attitude.

What information or message must I convey?

Have your facts in order before you begin to write. Eliminate unnecessary or nice-to-know information. Focus on the main message.

What results do I want?

What do you want your reader to do? How do you want your reader to respond? If you don't know, your reader won't know either.

CHECK YOURSELF

Read the text of the letter below. Answer each of the following questions.

Dear Ms Wales,

The National Association of Women in Business is holding its annual meeting on 15–18 January 1995, in London. As a successful female entrepreneur, we would like to invite you to be the main speaker at our closing banquet on 18 January at 7.30 P.M. in the ballroom of the Newland Hotel.

My assistant, Sarah Roderick, will ring you next week to learn whether this date is available and if you can accept the invitation.

We need to complete our planning within the next 30 days. On behalf of the planning committee, I would like to express our hope that you will be able to attend.

Yours sincerely,

Why was the letter written? Refer to the reasons for writing above. Which one applies to this letter?

_____

How well do you think the writer knows the reader?

Very well _____   Somewhat acquainted _____

Not personally acquainted _____   Not at all _____

Does the letter convey a warm, human attitude?

Yes _____   No _____   Not certain _____

What information was necessary? List the factors needed by the reader.

_____   _____

_____   _____

What results does the writer want? List the results the writer is seeking.

_____   _____

_____   _____

The solution appears at the end of the chapter.

PLANNING THE LETTER

Every successful letter begins with a plan. The plan may be a formal outline or, more typically, an informal list of the contents.

Planning your letter involves three steps:

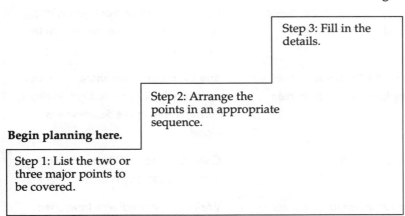

Begin writing here.

Step 3: Fill in the details.

Step 2: Arrange the points in an appropriate sequence.

Begin planning here.

Step 1: List the two or three major points to be covered.

Prescription for writer's block

The cure for writer's block is to *begin writing*. Use your letter plan and write a first draft. If time permits, put it aside and revise it later. The most experienced writers will tell you they write, rewrite and write again – before writing the final copy.

LETTER PARTS

Most letters contain either three or four parts, as appropriate:

- an opening or introduction
- the main message
- a statement of results desired
- the closing

The opening

Four critical seconds – business correspondence specialists tell us that's how long you have to get the attention of your reader with your opening.

The opening contains your topic sentence – your reason for writing. A dull opening suggests a dull letter – one that may not even be read, let alone generate a response.

Weak openings	**Improved openings**
We have received your letter of 25 June 199–, confirming your plans to speak to our group.	Thank you for confirming your plans to speak to our group.
Obvious fact. If you had not received a letter, would you be writing this one?	Combines a warm thank you with a brief statement of the purpose of the letter.
This letter is to inform you of the forthcoming Executive Committee meeting.	The Executive Committee will meet on Thursday 27 July at 2 P.M. in the Spring Room of the Southdowns Hotel.
Don't talk about it – do it!	Gives the reader all the important facts in the first paragraph
We have made attempts to collect the overdue amount on your account.	We are frustrated! We have tried unsuccessfully to collect the £159.15 owed us on your account no. 7QR54.
A good beginning but leaves out the facts.	An unusual opening that is sure to catch the attention of the reader. Leaves no doubt in the reader's mind about the purpose of the letter.

The main message

The main message contains all the necessary information and details you need to convey. It can be taken directly from a carefully written letter plan.

Weak main messages	**Improved main messages**
Jonathan Cookson was a student at Summerlin College during the late 1980s and early1990s.	Jonathan Cookson attended Summerlin College from September 1988 to June 1990. He gained an MPhil in Education.
Verifies the fact that he attended the college but gives few additional – and needed – details.	Gives detailed information about Jonathan's college experience.
Martin Wright is a former employee of Magna Services. His work was always excellent.	Martin Wright was employed by Magna Services as a systems analyst from 15 June 1985 to 30 September 1989. Martin's individual work was always superior, and his teamwork was excellent. We were sorry to lose him, but we understood his reasons for seeking another position.
Verifies his employment without giving any details. Would not be helpful to a potential employer.	Gives detailed information about Martin's employment. Adds a warm, personal note in the final sentence.

The action or results

When appropriate, state what information you are seeking or what results you desire. Be specific. Do not leave your reader wondering what you want.

Request for action or results	**Improved requests**
Please confirm your appointment as soon as possible.	Please confirm your appointment by calling my assistant on extension 2655 no later than Friday, 15 July.
States request vaguely. Does not give the reader the information needed to comply with the request.	States the action desired in definite terms.

The preliminary audit report would be helpful at our meeting next week.

Please bring the preliminary audit report with you when we meet the comptroller next week.

Suggests possible action rather than making a firm request.

States specifically what is needed and when it is needed.

The closing

The closing of your letter may take any of several forms, as determined by the nature of the letter. It may be a summary of the major ideas, a simple statement of goodwill or a clincher to motivate the reader.

Weak closings
Thank you in advance.

Improved closings
Thanks so much for your patience in this matter.

A presumptuous closing. Never assume the reader's action.

Combines an always appropriate thank you with a specific comment.

You can order this special communications package by calling us today.

A phone call from you will enable you to enjoy the advantages of on-line communications immediately.

The reader knows the product is available. This closing does nothing to clinch the deal.

This closing has the reader in mind. It is to the reader's advantage to place an order – a good clincher.

THE APPEARANCE OF YOUR LETTERS

Marie Peebles is a skilled letter writer. She plans each letter carefully before she writes it. She always reads her letters to be certain she has included all pertinent information. She makes a concentrated effort to stress the reader's point of view and writes with warm tones. Yet she often fails to get results, particularly when writing to people she does not know.

She took several samples of her writing to a communications consultant, who promptly identified her problem – the appearance of her letters. Marie was puzzled because the format of her letters was consistent with the format of letters found in her predecessor's files. She soon learned that her formatting skills were outdated.

PROJECTING A CONTEMPORARY IMAGE

What is appropriate formatting for today's business letters? What recent style changes can you incorporate into your letters to enhance their overall appearance? How can you send a non-verbal message that says you understand that both appearance and content contribute to successful business writing?

Someone once said, 'You never get a second chance to make a first impression.' That statement is true of your letters.

Writing for results involves not only the contents of a letter but also its appearance. Some readers may make a decision about whether or not to read your letter and respond to it solely on how it looks. Whether you are the originator of the letter or the support staff person who keys and prints the document, you must be aware of how a letter should look if it is to bring results.

Chapter 9 *Checklist*

✓ Did you begin with a writing plan?
✓ Did you limit each paragraph to one major idea?
✓ When possible, did you limit paragraphs to five or six lines each?
✓ Have you used listings for lengthy details rather than narratives?
✓ Did you remember that one-page letters are always preferable?
✓ Did you check all details before writing the final copy?
✓ Scan the letter. Is it placed attractively on the page? Does it appear balanced with your letterhead?
✓ Did you use the default margins of your software (usually one inch)?
✓ How readable is your letter?

CHECK YOURSELF SOLUTION

Page 108

Why was the letter written?
To inform.

How well do you think the writer knows the reader?
Not at all.

Does the letter convey a warm, human attitude?
Yes.

What information was necessary?
Invitation to speaker.
Audience, date, time, and place.
Information for response.

What results does the writer want?
A positive response to the invitation.

CHAPTER 10

Final Checks to Ensure Success

This chapter will help you to:
- **focus on the purpose of your document and the end results**
- **maintain a positive point of view**
- **focus on problems rather than personalities**
- **assume respect and goodwill among colleagues**

Several basic business attitudes can guide you as you write, speak, fax, or e-mail to your colleagues. These attitudes do not change from one kind of communication to another. They do not change from one decade to another.

KEEP YOUR EYE ON THE END RESULT

Whatever you are writing, use your purpose as your organizing principle. Do you want a manufacturer to refund your money? Do you want a subordinate to stop rolling in to work 10 minutes late?

Ask clearly for what you want. Never end a business communication that needs a response without actually stating what you want the reader to do.

This letter is an example of a poor end to a business communication.

---

10 June 1993

Mr Peter Ash
Fabrics International
22 Warehouse Lane
Portsmouth TQ5 7JE

Dear Peter,

We have been using your tent canvas for several years and until recently we were happy with what you delivered.

The last shipment of material we got from you, however, had several flaws. The colours were not consistent or bright and the final waterproofing coating was not as effective as you claimed. Our quality-control people tell us it leaks like a sieve when they do waterproofing checks. We cannot possibly use it for our tents unless we want to risk losing our own customers.

You know that we run on a tight schedule. Getting this bad canvas has meant that we cannot finish our tents and fill our own orders to our customers on time.

We feel you should respond to the problem immediately.

Yours sincerely,

Tom Post

This letter makes it clear that Tom and his colleagues are not happy with the material supplied by the manufacturer. It explains why. It gives details. But what is the manufacturer supposed to do about it? What does Tom want? Does he want his money back? Is he ending the relationship with the manufacturer? Does he want new material? Does he just want to complain?

If Tom does not tell Peter Ash precisely what he wants, Peter will have difficulty pleasing Tom.

Here is another way Tom could have dealt with the problem.

---

10 June 1993

Mr Peter Ash
Fabrics International
22 Warehouse Lane
Portsmouth TQ5 7JE

SUBJECT: Request for free replacement of defective material purchased 13 March 1992. Order no LI82729

Dear Peter,

I write to report some problems with the last shipment of material we ordered from you and to ask that your company replace the defective goods.

The last shipment of material had several flaws. The colours were not consistent or bright enough. When our quality-control people tested it they found that the final waterproof coating was not effective.

We know that this is not the norm for your tent material, which deserves its reputation as the best on the market. We assume you will be as anxious to correct this flaw as we are.

In the meantime, we are now behind schedule in tent production because we cannot proceed with the material you sent us. We feel confident that you will replace order no. LI82729 with non-defective material no later than 10 July.

If you cannot respond to our request and deadline, please contact me immediately.

I look forward to hearing from you, and to receiving the new material.

Yours sincerely,

Tom Post

In this letter, Tom makes it clear that he wants new material from the manufacturer by 10 July. He states that if a problem prevents Peter Ash from doing what he asks, Peter should contact him immediately. Tom lets the manufacturer know the urgency of the response time, but his tone is not hysterical or blaming.

Tom includes a subject line so that there is no doubt about what the letter is addressing. He places the order number in the subject line so that his order can be traced quickly. He makes it as easy for the manufacturer as he can.

Tom is very likely to get what he wants – a fast replacement for the defective shipment. He also gets a grateful supplier who will bend over backwards for him in the future because he did not cancel his account at the first tough point in their relationship. Tom is using this problem to build strong business ties.

THE POSITIVE POINT OF VIEW

Tom's positive tone is as important to his letter as its content. He makes sure that Peter Ash knows that he respects the manufacturer's work ('We know that this is not the norm for your tent material, which deserves its reputation as the best on the market'). More important, he lets Peter know he is confident that they agree on the problem's urgency ('We assume you will be as anxious to correct this flaw as we are'). Tom's tone is assured, professional and positive. It assumes that there is no difficulty that cannot be overcome.

Why is a positive tone so hard to achieve? Because in the push and shove of daily work, particularly work that is deadline sensitive or that is not going well, people feel anxious and defensive. They make the critical mistake of conveying these feelings to their readers. The communicator who passes on anxiety and blame generates anxiety and defensiveness. Anxious, defensive people do not do their best work. They cannot respond, and they cannot help you deal with your problems.

FOCUS ON THE PROBLEM, NOT THE PERSON

A good last check on any business communication is a quick search for 'I' and 'you'. If you find more than one sentence beginning with 'you', evaluate all of your sentences for tone. Have you shifted your attention to a person rather than the work at hand?

What kind of response would Tom have got had he written the following letter?

June 10 1993

Mr Peter Ash
Fabrics International
22 Warehouse Lane
Portsmouth TQ5 7JE

SUBJECT: Request for free replacement of defective material purchased 13 March 1992. Order no LI82729

Dear Peter,

Your last shipment to us was defective, and I write to ask you to replace the order and do something about your poor materials and irresponsible quality control.

Your people could not possibly have checked for waterproofing or colour, since both were defective. You did not see the problem and then you went ahead and shipped it off to us.

Your carelessness has jeopardized our own relationships with the customers who are waiting for the tents that we cannot make because of problems in your product.

I assume you will ship us a new, more carefully inspected replacement by 10 July. If you cannot do this, please contact me immediately.

Thank you for your prompt response. We look forward to receiving the new material.

Yours sincerely,

Tom Post

All the same points are made – the specific problems, the repercussions, the request for a replacement within a specified time – but the tone is very different.

Most people in Peter Ash's chair, reading this letter, would realize that Tom's problem is valid and requires attention. They would realize that Tom is not personally angry with *them* but is angry about the condition of the material. Yet the tone of this letter feels personal. Angry letters that feel personal tend to generate self-protective rather than productive responses.

If Peter Ash received this letter from Tom, his first concern might not be to solve the problem. It might be to protect his personal reputation and to vent a little anger at this person who seems furious with him.

RESPECT AND GOODWILL AMONG COLLEAGUES

In Chapter 5, we learned that people often 'mirror' the behaviour that is directed at them. If they are treated with respect, they treat their colleagues accordingly.

This is a basic tenet of successful communication and one of the hardest to follow. Ultimately, however, it is worth the effort because:

1. It improves the quality of everyday work life.
2. It builds productive and trusting work relationships.
3. It creates a work climate in which mistakes and problems can be honestly faced (and therefore solved).

This attitude is reflected in actual business writing through:

1. The steady use of the active voice.
2. The reliable use of facts and details, without evasions.
3. Little or no use of unnecessary, 'padding' language.

In short, problems are not hidden or avoided. They are faced. Facing problems means holding people responsible for the quality of their work. Respect and goodwill do not preclude holding individuals to the standards of their job. In fact, they demand it.

Chapter 10 *Checklist*

✓ Stick to your purpose – keep your messages direct and clear.
✓ Avoid negative, accusatory endings.
✓ Keep a positive point of view.
✓ Be careful not to put your reader on the defensive.
✓ Focus on problems, not personalities.
✓ Remember that you want to work *with* the reader, not prove a point or place blame.
✓ Assume respect and goodwill among colleagues.

Test Yourself

Congratulations! You have just taken another important step in your professional development by completing *Successful Business Writing*.

This test is provided as a quick means of reinforcing the material you have just covered.

Approximate time to complete: 15 minutes

INSTRUCTIONS: Circle the letter of the correct answer.

1. Which of the following are good reasons for writing a business letter?
   a. To avoid conveying embarrassing information by phone.
   b. To respond to an enquiry.
   c. To prove one's worth to the employer by generating paperwork.
   d. To avoid a personal contact.

2. If you have difficulty getting started when writing, the best solution is to:
   a. Prepare a draft copy.
   b. Put it off until the end of the day after your other work is done.
   c. Begin writing.
   d. Write a final copy on your first try to make up for lost time.

3. The beginning of the letter is important because:
   a. It identifies you as the writer.
   b. Dull openings are seldom recouped later.
   c. You have four seconds to gain your reader's attention.
   d. Most people never read the last part of the letter.

4. The proper sequence for writing a letter or memo is:
   a. Plan, arrange, fill in details and write.
   b. Plan and write.
   c. Gather details, make a plan and write.
   d. Write individual paragraphs, arrange them in proper sequence and rewrite.

5. Which of the following closings would be most appropriate for a sales letter?
   a. You are a phone call away from enjoying your new widget!
   b. If you want to order a widget, please ring me.
   c. Widgets cost only £9.95 each.
   d. We hope you will seriously consider purchasing a widget soon.

6. The readability of your letter involves:
   a. The reading level.
   b. The amount of friendliness that emanates from your writing.
   c. The overall appearance of your letter.
   d. The number of paragraphs you have used.

7. The most critical question you can ask yourself before writing is:
   a. Who am I writing to?
   b. What do I want the reader to know or do after reading this letter/memo?
   c. Who else might read this?
   d. When should I write?

8. One of the secrets of successful memos is:
   a. Say only what is necessary.
   b. Keep the length to two or three paragraphs.
   c. Write as often as necessary until you are certain the message is understood.
   d. Write a friendly last paragraph.

9. Electronic messages differ from memos in which of the following ways?
   a. Since they are transmitted via computer, their importance is understood.
   b. The language of electronic messages is more succinct.
   c. It is never necessary to keep a hard copy.
   d. They are more personal.

10. Conciseness, one of the five C's of business writing, is:
    a. Using long words and repeating words as necessary.
    b. Writing as briefly as possible.
    c. Eliminating excess and long words, as well as redundant expressions.
    d. Presenting all the facts.

11. You can achieve clarity in your writing by:
    a. Using jargon, so the reader understands your position.
    b. Controlling the number of paragraphs.
    c. Avoiding the use of vague language and jargon.
    d. Writing very short sentences.

12. Which of the following sentences applies the write-for-results principles?
    a. At a later date we will review our position.
    b. Thank you in advance for your co-operation.
    c. We are certain you can never understand our position.
    d. Your concerns are our concerns.

13. A condescending tone in writing is:
    a. Sometimes necessary in order to convey the message.
    b. A matter of tone rather than words.
    c. Writing at an elementary reading level.
    d. Avoiding the use of big words.

14. Which of the following sentences is grammatically correct?
    a. Neither Mary or John wishes to give up their secretary.
    b. Every one of the members is planning to participate.
    c. The three manager's offices are being renovated.
    d. There is a number of people who have not responded.

15. Which of the following sentences contains no spelling errors?
    a. The controller said the major capitol commitment was a positive step.
    b. Melinda Jones will supercede Richard Gray next month.
    c. We are unable to accomodate your request at this time.
    d. Your recommendation is accepted.

16. Clarify the following:

at the present time   _____

due to the fact that   _____

in order that   _____

with regard to   _____

utilize   _____

visualize   _____

in the near future   _____

ascertain   _____

concur   _____

facilitate   _____

endeavour (as a verb)   _____

in close proximity   _____

17. Identify two strengths that the active voice can give your writing.

_____

_____

18. Identify three specific strategies for getting down to work quickly as a writer.

_____

_____

19. How many ideas can a paragraph typically address gracefully?

_____

_____

20. Identify two characteristics of a successful, businesslike 'tone'.

_____

_____

21. Identify two techniques that help organize ideas on paper.

_____

_____

22. What is the most important question writers can ask themselves about the memo, report or letter they are developing?

_____

_____

23. Identify two questions other than the one you gave in Question 22 that can guide a writer's work.

_____

_____

24. What specific steps can a writer take when stuck in the middle of a writing task?

_____

_____

25. Identify two specific techniques any writer can use to ensure that his or her letters or memos get the kinds of responses desired.

_____

_____

ANSWERS

1. *b*	6. *a*	11. *c.*
2. *c*	7. *a*	12. *a*
3. *b*	8. *a*	13. *b*
4. *a*	9. *b*	14. *b*
5. *a*	10. *c*	15. *d*

16. now; because; so; about, use; see, imagine; soon; learn; agree; make easier; try; near.

17. Maintains a brisk and controlled pace; makes your message clearer.

18. Arrange your work space in ways that make you comfortable and signal that it is now time to work; visualize your entire task before beginning; break the task, if it is large, into smaller parts.

19. One.

20. Courtesy; brevity.

21. Outlining; brainstorming.

22. Why am I writing this?

23. Who is reading this? What must I say to my reader to get my desired result or reaction?

24. Walk away from your desk; think about something else. If that doesn't help, note all the things that attract your attention, sit down again and examine what attracted your attention, and ask yourself if it throws any light on why you got stuck, or how to continue your document. Change outlining techniques or strategies. Just write – do not edit or stop yourself. Conduct a self-interview to focus your purpose. Create a form that guides your thinking by asking you basic questions about your end purpose.

25. Focus on the problem, not on personalities; maintain a positive tone. (Other acceptable answers include: write clearly; write concisely; maintain a clear attitude of co-operation and respect.)